The Changing Culture of Leadership:

Women Leaders' Voices

Acknowledgements

We owe a debt of gratitude to many people for their contributions to this publication. First and foremost, our thanks go to the fifty-two women leaders who generously gave us their time and support for this project. Their openness during the interviews has lent an unusual richness, depth and power to our research.

Our sincere thanks go to our colleagues at The Change Partnership Ltd and the Tavistock Consultancy Service, who have made available to us the time, thinking space and funds to accomplish this research and writing; and for their unstinting support in so many ways.

The support team at CPL has worked cheerfully behind the scenes sorting seemingly endless administrative details, and we are very grateful to them.

Our thanks also to Phil Kay, Barbara Shore, Stephanie Lewis, Anne Limb, Barbara Salter, Nicky Mayhew and Bill Nickerson, as well as our partners and friends, who provided much-valued help and good advice in our design and editorial processes.

First published 1999
by The Change Partnership Limited
Egyptian House, 170 Piccadilly
London W1V 9DD

Designed and typeset by Phil Kay Design,
Saffron Walden, Essex CB11 4LT

Produced in Great Britain by EXP Group
Ltd, Hemel Hempstead, Herts HP2 7DA

ISBN 0-9537535-0-6 (pbk)

CONTENTS

INTRODUCTION

A case for change?

Most large corporations and organisations (from central government to public sector to professional services) already recruit male and female graduates year on year in roughly equal proportions, and many have done so for a couple of decades. As long ago as 1990, approximately one in five of all of the UK's 'middle management' stratum was female. The great majority of the new jobs which will be created in the next five years in the UK will be filled by women – perhaps to the tune of 70% or even 80%. Yet in spite of this, few women make it to the top of medium-to-large organisations in the UK. Astonishingly, as we arrive at the third Millennium, less than three per cent of the executive directors of Britain's quoted companies are female. In large organisations the situation is even more extreme, with women making up less than one per cent of the executive directors of FTSE 100 companies. Does this matter?

"LADIES AND GENTLEMEN ... THE CUSTOMER!"

We believe it does. Apart from the arguments based on social justice, it is beginning to matter at the strategic level, and we believe that organisations which persist in the belief that somehow, in some way not fully determined, at some indeterminate time in the future, more women will find their way to the top jobs are running increasing strategic risks. It was this perception which originally prompted the research upon which this Report draws. Is there a strategic business case for more women at the top? Let us make just four points.

First, to state the obvious, the world has changed, and is going to go on changing – almost certainly at a much faster rate in the first decade of the twenty-first century than at any time in the lifetime of today's directors and senior managers. Globalisation of markets (and thus competition), the burgeoning of e-commerce, the pace of technological and business convergence, the breadth and depth of strategic partnerships are combining to create a new situation where it is almost impossible to predict future developments accurately, even a few years away. The effects of all this wash through all organisations – not just those in the business front-line, but also through government, public services and the professions. At the same time, a social revolution is going on, hand-in-hand with these business changes. People's expectations of how they wish to work, how they view careers, and indeed what they want from life itself are changing just as rapidly, and just as unpredictably. All of this puts a premium on identifying how markets are changing, and being able to deploy resources rapidly to follow those changes.

In turn, this need for agility and sharper focus has created powerful drivers for change in the way people build organisational structures. There is a steady shift away from the traditional 'command and control' hierarchies towards greater flexibility, and organisations which are more directly linked to the market and the final customer. This has huge implications for organisational cultures, many of which are not measuring up to the demands which are now starting to be placed on them. The need is for flexible deployment (and employment) to be able to deploy people faster and more flexibly, in teams which combine together and disband or re-form in line with changes in their organisation's external environment. Within this blur of change, evidence is beginning to emerge which supports the thesis that having more women at the top of organisations makes it easier to move organisations in the required directions.

Second, it may be a truism, but any organisation which fails to listen to its customers will not long survive. Rather more than half of the people in the general population in the developed world are women. Women are in many respects the key consumers in today's post-industrial society, for (as one of our interviewees said): "the power of the purse has shifted to us". This is not just in the obvious, traditionally female markets. Tom Peters in his book *The Circle of Innovation* (1997) reports that 57% of motor tyres sold in the US are purchased by women! Women's economic power has increased hugely in the last quarter century, and is set to grow even faster in the next. Even when the women may not be wielding the credit cards themselves, their influence on major buying decisions is significant – for example, on an increasing proportion of leisure and recreational spending; on their partners' clothes and other 'style' items; and on almost all family and home-related purchases from food and furnishings to cars, computers and keep fit equipment. As traditional family units continue to give way to more ad hoc arrangements in society, and in particular as more and more homes become 'single adult occupied', women's economic power will grow in leaps and bounds. Organisations increasingly need a mix of people at the top of their management structures who can reflect the reality of the market places they serve: people who think the way their customers think, in fact. Those who get this right by creating a more diverse mix of talent at the top will undoubtedly reap handsome rewards. Those who continue to under-utilise half of the human race are more likely to falter. Creating high performance organisations is difficult enough per se, and self-induced handicapping by the exclusion of women at the top (even if unconsciously) is not the most promising of positions from which to enter the new millennium!

Third, it is becoming ever more apparent that the quality of the performance of people in an organisation matters. What separates the best performing organisations from the 'also-rans' is not just about the mechanics of the business. It is about how good an organisation's people are, about how well they are led and motivated, and how well they are integrated into their team, and into the organisation as a whole. It is increasingly obvious that so-called 'soft skills' are essential to world-class performance. Virtually all academic business thinking now places significant emphasis on such skills as engaging and motivating staff; on celebrating the successful long-term development of people and teams; and on having relationship and team-building driven by an overt value set which has the recognition and valuing of individual difference at its centre; in short, of winning the hearts and minds of people in the organisation and, having won them, harnessing them to the benefit of the organisation.

Alongside this resurgence of interest in the primacy of people management skills there is a growing acknowledgement that women may possess these essential 'people skills' in a greater depth than men. This is a generalisation, and of course it is important not to be doctrinaire about this – many men possess well-developed 'soft' skills, too. It seems remarkable, therefore, that at a time when so many organisations are taking a renewed interest in changing their culture, and in managing in ways which produce significantly higher quality performance from ordinary mortals, there is still so little use being made of women's talents. From any viewpoint it is remarkable that so few women are in positions at the top of organisations, and the remedy seems obvious. It becomes even more obvious when one considers the number of women recruited into organisations who leave in mid-career, not so much for the sake of starting families (as is often cited, by way of an excuse for having very few senior women!) as because they simply do not find the organisation suits their aspirations, skills sets and, in many cases, their values. This is the most enormous waste of money, resources and scarce talent – and requires only a shift in mind-set at the top of the organisation to reverse.

Finally, and to add some urgency to these themes, it is interesting to reflect on the situation today in medium and large organisations in the US. It is often said that trends which become mainstream in the US arrive here shortly afterwards, so it is worth noting that (per Catalyst's Census of Women Board Directors of the Fortune 500, 1998) in the top quintile of the Fortune 500, 97% of companies had one women Director on their Board; and 67% had two or more women Directors. These are the companies with which the leading European and UK companies must compete in rapidly globalising markets, and the position of many UK FTSE 100 companies only seems to make sense if one believes that the Fortune 100 companies have it wrong. This is a serious issue, and organisations in the UK should worry a great deal more about this phenomenon than they do currently. Failing to select for top talent from the full pool of talent available – failure that is in taking pains to support the development of women for top roles, and being bold enough to appoint them to those roles – looks strategically dangerous, if not downright suicidal.

This Report looks deep into the experiences of some of the few women who have made it to the top, and sets out to present those experiences in the hope that they will provide insights and spurs to action not just from women with leadership aspirations, but even more importantly from the (largely male) leaders of today who can make the necessary changes happen – and thus it is to those male leaders that this Report is targeted.

Executive summary

• In 1990 a Hansard Society Commission Report revealed, in a survey of 144 of the CBI's top 200 firms, plus ten major building societies, 81% had no women on their holding boards; 58% had no women on either their main or subsidiary boards; and 22% had one woman on either their main or subsidiary board. The Commission concluded that "if boardrooms are where power and influence reside, then women are clearly excluded", but anticipated that the 1990s offered potential for change.

• In 1999 the situation has not significantly changed. Within the FTSE 100, the total number of directors (male and female executive and non-executive) is 1178; only 69 of those appointments are held by women. Some women hold more than one, so the actual number of women (as opposed to directorships held by women) is 61. Of the 61 women who hold Board director positions, 53 are non-executive directors. There are only eight women FTSE 100 executive directors. Across all of Britain's publicly listed companies only 3.32% of non-executive directors, and 2.67% of executive directors, are women.

• In both public and private sectors, women remain under-represented in senior positions at the very top of organisations where strategy is set, where decisions are made, and where organisational cultures are shaped. This leaves the upper echelons of organisational life mono-dimensional, and has only a detrimental impact upon the ability of top teams to formulate rounded strategies to meet the needs of its customer base - which in many sectors is more than 50% female.

• Recruiting and retaining high-performing executive women has an impact, for the better, upon the performance of the organisation.

Skills and attributes

• Women executives feel as much at home with the 'hard' issues of business – the numbers – as they do with the people issues. There was no sense in which 'soft' skills prevailed, especially not at the expense of delivering the bottom line.

• Building committed and loyal teams was seen as the means of delivery of hard objectives – with the softer skills being used to great effect in that team-building process. There was a genuine passion among women leaders for building 'the best team'.

- There was some modesty about their own skills and talents, which could easily lead (particularly in a 'macho' environment) to those being overlooked. Their modesty – coupled with a desire to give their teams the credit – was a marked trait.

- "Playing politics" was frowned upon, and disliked. Most of the women saw it as irrelevant and destructive, especially where it hampered team-building or delivery.

Leadership style and values

- An important part of the value set was the importance of caring about people in the organisation. It is this overt value which produces the high degree of loyalty from their teams.

- None of the women found difficulty with the notion of being tough. Most saw it as part of the requirement for a top job, but were firmly of the view that it was not necessary to be unpleasant to be tough.

- They placed emphasis on clear, open leadership, where their own personal values were transparent to the organisation. This was a source of great pride, and strength – there was no separation of business and personal value set.

- All saw the encouragement of creativity as a vital part of leadership, and linked this to the need for them to act as role models and to inspire.

- We were struck, time and again, by the similarity between what the women said about their own leadership style and priorities, and the changes in leadership styles advocated by many of today's leading management thinkers.

- There was a sense of these women's leadership style being ahead of its time.

Contributory factors to leadership styles

- Home background, and in particular the support of parents, was an important ingredient. Many of the women leaders had been challenged to achieve to their full potential when young.

- Education, too, was important. Emphasis was placed on the importance of single-sex education, not least because this was more likely to establish clearer role models.

- Much importance was given to the truly important drivers in their lives.

Caring about people came high on the list, linked with a strong commitment to personal development – a sense in which it was a leader's duty to nurture and encourage others to achieve their full potential.

- There was also a sense of a life-long quest for excellence – a striving measured against absolute measures.

- The striving for perfection led many of the women to set exceptionally high standards and goals for themselves – but also underpinned a sustained drive to deliver.

- Money per se was not seen as the prime motivator. It was nice to have, but not an end in itself, and was seen as much less important than factors such as competing successfully for outcomes, having their teams succeed, opportunities for learning, reaching difficult goals, etc.

Unplanned career paths

- Very few of the women had planned their careers, and most felt it was of less importance than demonstrating achievement and character, and letting that speak for their readiness for bigger roles.

- A powerful determination to "seize the day" was also apparent. Luck was acknowledged as playing its part, but there was a recognition of the need to be able to recognise the lucky breaks when they occurred.

- Being less "political" may also mean less time spent in plotting their own way forward, and there was some sense that women's apparently greater willingness to admit to doubts or uncertainties may be a career handicap at times.

- Girls' general conditioning in society with an emphasis placed on tempering overt aggression or strong self assertion in favour of preserving and equalising, may make it much harder for women to be comfortable in organisations with strongly male characteristics. This too may have a significant influence on career paths.

Career helps

- All saw the support and understanding of partners as being important in pursuing a top career, and absolutely essential where children were involved.

- Most of the women leaders interviewed had children.

- Role models were important in theory, but often (particularly later in careers) came a recognition that there were few role models for aspiring top women.

- This tended to make mentoring and coaching a significant activity. Many of the women leaders acknowledged a debt to a coach or mentor (often a more experienced male colleague) at important points in their careers.

- Being the only woman in a senior position in an organisation made for very high visibility, and this was not always a comfortable experience, though it was acknowledged that it did have the advantage of making success very visible.

Career 'blockers'

- Some of the women described "a lack of self-confidence" as a difficulty. This often translated as a feeling of embarrassment at the thought of 'blowing one's own trumpet'. It was felt that this came more naturally to males – thus putting men at a clear advantage in a male-oriented organisational culture.

- Another difficulty was the lack of natural networks for senior women, a direct result of their scarcity in organisations. A particular frustration was felt where networking was made to equate to 'male bonding' in the organisation, and took place (for example) on the golf course or in the pub, since this could result in exclusion of senior women.

- It was felt that balance between work and home life was extremely difficult to sustain. There was little doubt that the pressure to achieve a satisfactory balance pushed women towards sub-optimising careers, though that could be avoided by the organisation's recognition of the issue, and the taking of measures to help. Most organisations had some way to go in this

- Envy had been a problem in a number of the women's careers, though the women recognised this was an issue which could arise for anyone in a pre-eminent position, male or female – and the envious could be of either gender.

The impact of organisational culture

- Being a lone female voice in a large organisation (as was the case with many of the women leaders) was an experience which produced mixed emotions. On the one hand, there was for some a sense of excitement in being the lone woman in a position of power. The more prevalent view was that being in such a position was a great additional burden to a busy senior manager.

- It was interesting to contrast this (being a "lone voice") with the much more positive feelings associated with being one of several women in a better 'gender-balanced' team. The implication was that it was easier for women to achieve their full potential as Directors in circumstances where they were not the only women in post.

- Women leaders were deeply appreciative of senior people in the organisation who had deliberately set out to create an atmosphere in which diversity would flourish. It was clear that cultures which were managed with the intent of making it easier to develop senior women were richer in many respects.

- Quite apart from being the "lone voice" the women leaders were also acutely aware that simply by virtue of their scarcity in top roles women who got to the top would always be spotlighted in the public eye in a way that would be rare for their male colleagues.

- Some bolder spirits saw this 'spotlight' as something positive, to be used as leverage in their careers. Many of the women believed they could deal with media attention, even where it was "justified" only by their gender.

- Within these (sometimes conflicting) currents, the most difficult issue the women identified was that of coping with cultures in which they always were the "lone voice", "the one in the spotlight", or, more bluntly, the "outsider". This has little to do with business, but a lot to do with persistence of traditional male dominated cultures in UK organisations.

- In contrast to this difficulty of being "the perpetual alien" in the local culture, there was also a keen awareness about the power of the history and traditions of their organisations. This was coupled with an excitement that they were in a position to contribute to changing the historic culture, of taking a constructive role in building something better from the legacy. It was graphically described by one interviewee as "an old world order dying, as a new one was being born". This was a strongly positive feeling.

- In one way, the women leaders saw themselves as privileged, since their very novelty at the most senior tables meant they were inevitably seen as part of the new order, simply because they were definitively not part of the old.

- This did not necessarily make culture change easier. There was recognition that some early, successful women succeeded because they out-competed the men at their own game. It was clear that this was not what today's women leaders wanted for themselves or the next generation. They wanted to be accepted as women, not as substitute men.

- Progress was being made, but it was slow.

- Male attitudes still shape most UK organisations.

- Almost all of the women leaders had ambitions to change the cultures around them, and many favoured some form of "balanced score-card" approach as a more rounded way of evaluating success and of driving performance.

- Those working in organisations using only key financial ratios found the experience frustrating, not because they had any difficulties with the hard numbers, but because they saw this narrow focus as missing out on the measurement of many elements of strategic importance to the organisation.

Changing the culture

- There was a widespread belief that most of the big waves of management change of the past decade had been basically reactive, and that there was now a pressing need in UK organisations to be more proactive. In particular, the need was to create cultures where team-work, creativity and innovation can thrive.

- It was clear that the women leaders had a sense of mission in this area, and were conscious of their potential to drive change in organisational cultures. They were also well aware that they were themselves, by their presence in the top team, a highly visible signal of change.

- The cultures aspired to were less political, and much less status-conscious; flatter; more caring; reliant more upon listening than telling; and (above all) sufficiently self-confident to allow people to make their own judgements and decisions.

- This was a highly developmental vision – one in which close hierarchical control gives way to values-driven, more responsive networking structures.

- Most recognised a language difference between themselves and their male colleagues.

- The development of new cultural norms was seen as the key to the future. The women leaders saw themselves as pioneers of a paradigm shift in cultures, and role models for 'the New Leadership' styles required post-2000.

My baby's worth more than my £1/4m salary

Mother love – it's the real thing

Penny Hughes

Women still face uphill trek to place on board

Women fight for pension rights

Women put pressure on the glass ceiling

The number of female executives may be rising, but their progress to the boardroom is still slow, the survey shows

Why women make better managers

'I felt so mistreated by male colleagues that I just had to resign'

Dixons recruits 'superwoman'

Bye-bye baby, I'm off to work again

Women on course for top posts in management

Extending the shelf life of women

Chapter 1

What is this research about?

- Women in leadership positions in 1990
- Ten years on: how much has changed?
- Watching an old world dying – and a new one struggling to be born ...
- The contribution of this research

This section summarises the origins of our research on Women Leaders and sets it in context; linking it to an earlier study of senior women in public and professional life. It outlines the findings of that earlier analysis and examines how much has changed; it introduces the key findings of our own research, and sets out the issues for debate on how to promote more diversity in the leadership of organisations in the UK.

1 What is this research about?

Women in leadership positions in 1990

Some ten years ago the Hansard Society for Parliamentary Government published a Report, Women at the Top. The Society had a practice of setting up commissions to report on subjects associated with the functioning of Parliamentary government. This report, **Women at the Top**, resulted from concerns that

"the under-representation of women in the upper reaches of public life in this country ... is a serious anomaly" *(1)*

The Commission (chaired by Lady Howe) concluded that it would be wrong to consider public life solely within the narrow confines of Parliament and government. It therefore looked at other areas, including the universities and business, from which the leadership of the country is drawn. The Commission's mandate was:

"To identify barriers to the appointment of women to senior occupational positions, and to other positions of power and influence, and to make recommendations as to how these barriers could be overcome."

The mandate was underpinned by a conviction that equality of representation of men and women in British institutions in both public and private sectors was a desirable thing on grounds both of social justice and economic efficiency. The commitment to achieving social justice via the principles of inclusion and equal representation is clearly articulated in the Report:

"Women at the top of professional and public life have an important role to play in changing society's attitudes towards women in the workplace as well as in other positions of power and influence, and in shaping decisions of great public importance."

The Commission was convinced there was clear economic benefit from increasing the number of women in corporate leadership positions. Predicting that at the end of the decade (that is, now) the labour market would be experiencing a shortage of talent, the Commissioners observed:

"Women are a under-utilised resource ... companies which adopt and publicise management development practices that benefit women's careers will have a distinct advantage in recruitment and gain an important edge over their competitors" *(1a)*

When the Commission examined the position of women's representation in management, the picture appeared encouraging. In the two previous decades women's representation had been increasing slowly but steadily. In 1971 women made up less than 5% of general management staff. In 1988 this had increased to 11%. Almost two-thirds of women in management (in 1990) had middle-rank status, representing one in five of all middle managers.

In senior management, in leadership positions, the Commission found a less optimistic situation. It found that up-to-date information about the representation of women on the boards of holding companies in Britain was "quite scarce". The Commission sought information from 144 of the top 200 CBI firms and ten major building societies. The survey revealed that 81% of those corporations had no women on their holding boards; 58% had no women on either their main or subsidiary boards; and 22% had one woman on either their main or subsidiary boards. The Commission concluded that

"if Boardrooms are where power and influence reside, then women are clearly excluded."

Women at the Top highlighted the existence of two significant barriers to women's optimum participation in the workplace: getting women into senior management, and getting women into the boardroom. The Commissioners observed that these "seemingly impenetrable barriers ... are only just being recognised, however, and largely remain to be tackled". They were optimistic about the potential for change, primarily because of the anticipated impact of demographic trends:

"The 1990s offer an opportunity for change. Eighty per cent of new workers in the next five years will be women, most of whom will have major family responsibilities. This, together with the creation of more high-level jobs, will compel employers to compete more strongly for the best candidates for their companies, irrespective of gender" *(1b)*

Ten years on: how much has changed?

The statistics in **Women at the Top** – from 154 top firms from ten years ago – are important because they provide a benchmark against which progress may be evaluated. Are the skills and experience of women now (to quote from the Hansard Society Commission Report) "being harnessed for the benefit of our society as a whole"? Are companies "gaining an important edge over their competitors through adopting and publicising management development practices that benefit women's careers"? And how much further forward are organisations in appointing women to leadership positions?

The answers to those questions present a mixed but fascinating picture. On the positive side, there is no doubt that women have continued to make inroads into junior and middle managerial positions, in both public and private sector.

In the public sector the numbers of women in positions of responsibility continue to rise. In the Civil Service, one of the largest employers in the UK, and in which women represent 51% of all non-industrial staff, the proportion of women employees at all senior levels has increased since 1984 *(2)*. Women represent 48% of all staff at Executive Officer level (the first management level) in comparison with 29% in 1984. In the Senior Civil Service *(3)* women now make up 18% of staff. At the responsibility level of the Senior Civil Service (which includes staff outside the SCS but with similar responsibilities, including senior Diplomatic Service staff) women represented 16% of staff in 1998 compared with 6% in 1984.

In both public and private sector it is a different story at the very top of organisations where strategic decisions are made. At the top of the Civil Service, for example, women are scarce. Just 2 of 19 Permanent Secretaries are women, and in the public sector more widely – health, education, local government – whilst there are many women in management roles there are still relatively few at the top levels (e.g. 97 women principals in 433 Further Education colleges). In the FTSE 100 companies which are, together with government spending, the main engines of the UK economy, a similar pattern emerges. In 1990, the appointment of women to board level was a recent phenomenon. The overwhelming majority of both executive and non-executive women directors had been appointed since 1986. Only two women had been appointed prior to 1980. Ten years on, with women in top management posts no longer 'a recent phenomenon', the picture at board level appears not very much changed.

Within the FTSE 100 companies the total number of directors (male and female) is 1178; and 69 of those appointments at board level are held by women. Some women however hold more than one appointment, so the actual number of women (as opposed to directorships held by women) is 61. Of the 61 women who hold Board director positions, there are 8 executive directors and 53 non-executive directors. Across all of Britain's publicly listed companies 3.32% of non-executive directors and 2.67% of executive directors, are women *(4)*.

In relation to their presence in the workforce *(5)* therefore, although in the ten years since the publication of the Hansard Society Commission Report there has been some progress, women are still under-represented in both public and private sectors in senior positions at the strategy-making levels, where the crucial decisions are made and where organisational cultures are shaped. This has the effect of leaving the upper echelons of organisational life looking largely mono-dimensional and of allowing organisational culture, behaviours, success criteria and organisational strategy to be determined by an homogeneous group. This has a detrimental impact upon the ability of the top team to formulate strategies which ensure that the organisation addresses effectively the needs of all its employee base and, even more importantly, its customer base, which in many sectors is well over 50% female *(6)*.

Watching an old world dying, and a new one struggling to be born ...

Ten years ago, many commentators thought that incremental change, pushed by shifting demographics, would inexorably produce greater diversity at senior levels. This has not happened and it is now clear that the model of incremental change was wrong. We are in an era of "Big Change" *(7)*. The paradigm has shifted and it seems unlikely that we will see a shift back to an era of measured, incremental change in our lifetime. The impact of globalisation, the development of e-commerce, mergers and acquisitions, technological convergence and strategic partnerings has irrevocably changed our world.

Organisations are being forced to re-think radically the way they operate in this new world. There has been a shift of power from producer to purchaser, from supply-driven to demand-led. Within this last shift, it is apparent that the demand is now coming from different sectors of the economy – from women, for example, who have dramatically increased their purchasing power as a result of their prominence in the workforce. This trend continues. *(8)*

Organisations are struggling to keep up. They know they need to be agile, innovative and fast moving to succeed. The best among them know they need to use their people differently. They know they need a changed paradigm of leadership.

The contribution of this research

This book – **The Changing Culture of Leadership: Women Leaders' Voices** – contributes to the definition of a new leadership paradigm. It is the first major study since the original 1990 Hansard Society Commission Report. It is important because it draws upon the hitherto largely invisible experience of fifty-two women who are today exercising organisational leadership in our new world, and asks some challenging questions about how they exercise that leadership. It focuses tightly on the experience of women who have made it to the top of their respective organisations in the UK.

... AND IT IS THANKS TO MY TEAM THAT I AM HERE TODAY

There are three key findings:

1. These women describe their leadership style in a very particular way. They appear to place especial emphasis upon a combination of effectiveness with people, and achievement of the task of the organisation. That is, they attach as much importance to the so-called "web of inclusion" *(9)* and good human relationships as they do to excellence in professional performance. The reason this is significant is because they are actually practising the kind of leadership described by almost all leading management thinkers and writers as essential for the success of organisations in the twenty-first century.

2. Despite being manifestly very successful high-achievers in their leadership roles, some of these women described unplanned career progress in which they were re-active rather than pro-active in seeking opportunities. This was combined in some cases with a lack of personal confidence.

   This apparent lack of confidence may be influenced by the women's upbringing, and (equally plausibly) by their experience of being in organisations, for most of their careers, where initiatives to change the culture to a more 'inclusive' style may not have been welcomed. On the other hand, the qualities of letting others have a share of the limelight, and of fostering the growth of confidence in their subordinates appear to be the other side of the coin, and these have helped the women develop particular skills in collaborative management, and in building highly effective teams. It is of course these skills which make them so valuable in their current leadership roles. It is also perhaps worth saying that women are more open about their self-perceived shortcomings than are men, and this finding is of significance to those seeking to develop 'high-flying' women.

3. Most of these women are working in organisational cultures which they had no hand in shaping, and which they frequently experience as inhospitable when taking up leadership roles. Perhaps because of this, they seem to be more alert to the necessity of building hospitable corporate cultures. As a consequence they have ideas about how organisational cultures may be changed to provide effective working environments for both men and women.

The findings are primarily qualitative rather than quantitative, and draw upon the wide range of sector and functional experience of women at the highest level in their field. *(10)* The book draws out the themes that have emerged from the analysis of these women's experience of leadership. It sets out a new contribution to the debate on diversity in leadership, and, in the final Chapter, sets out some prompts for a way forward, aimed at three audiences, viz:

- **Government:** Government is seeking to set an example of best practice in terms of female participation at leadership levels, both as an employer and as leader of the public sector. It is producing targets and league tables for itself, and for the rest of the public sector. The findings of research described here, the first of its kind for several years, will supplement government data, and provide a factual and detailed picture of women's experience at leadership levels, which may help inform policymaking.

- **Chairmen, Chief Executives and Boards:** Top executives increasingly ask what they may do to address the diversity issue, and what they need to do both to attract and retain high-performing women executives in their ranks. Our findings provide tangible evidence of what helps and hinders women in the exercise of leadership roles, and will assist organisations wishing to remove the barriers and enhance the factors which enable women's progress.

- **Individuals:** Effective leaders, male and female, want to give of their best, and support and learn from one another. The findings of this research suggest practical actions that they may take to find synergistic ways to work and lead in their organisations.

The ethical arguments in favour of equality of opportunity have been won. The issue is not about whether women should be equal. It is about what may be done to foster the conditions where genuine equality can be created. It will take energy, effort and imagination on the part of each of these groups to achieve a significant impact. The findings of our research suggest that there is a series of practical initiatives that policy-makers and leaders in the public and private sectors may take to help UK organisations accelerate the pace of change, and build organisational cultures in which able, high-performing women may thrive and make their optimum contribution, whatever the purpose or business of the organisation may be.

References: Chapter 1

(1) Report of The Hansard Society Commission on Women at the Top (1990) The Hansard Society London

(1a) ibid p 52

(1b) ibid p 2

(2) All statistics on the Civil Service from *Equal Opportunities in the Civil Service: Data Summary* (1998)

(3) The Senior Civil Service (SCS) was introduced on 1 April 1996. It covers most staff in former grades 2 to 5

(4) Total director population of men and women is 1178 excluding officers, e.g. Company Secretaries. All data from Hemmington Scott, August 1999

(5) 52% in September 1999, quoted at Labour Party Conference September 1999

(6) Some examples from the US economy: Women = 43% of Americans with assets > $500,000;

- three out of four healthcare decisions are made by women;
- two-thirds of healthcare dollars are spent by women;
- percentage of choices to buy a product that are made or decisively influenced by women:

Home furnishings:	95%
Holidays:	92%
Homes:	91%
Bank Account (choice of new):	89%
Medical Insurance:	88%

(Australian research)

Peters, Tom: *The Circle of Innovation* (1997) (pp396-398) Hodder & Stoughton London

(7) Taffinder, P (1998) *Big Change: a route map for corporate transformation.* John Wiley Chichester

(8) Henley Centre for Forecasting, *Planning for Social Change* 1994-5. (1995) The Henley Centre, London

(9) Helgesen, S: *The Web of Inclusion* (1995) Doubleday New York. Examination by an American author of how women's leadership styles transform organisations

(10) Not all the women are main board directors, though many are (see Chapter 2)

My baby's worth more than my £¼m salary

It's a classic dilemma of our time

Mother love – it's the real thing

Penny Hughes

Women still face uphill trek to place on board

Women fight for pension rights

Women put pressure on the glass ceiling

The number of female executives may be rising, but their progress to the boardroom is still slow, the survey shows

In the final extract from her book, …

Why women make better managers

…ects on the people who inspired her throughout her career

'I felt so mistreated by male colleagues that I just had to resign'

Dixons recruits 'superwoman'

Bye-bye baby, I'm off to work again

Women on course for top posts in management

Extending the shelf life of women

Chapter 2

Fifty-two women leaders

- About the women leaders
- Carrying out the research
- What the research is – and what it is not

In this section we describe the roles fulfilled by the women leaders we interviewed, the types of organisation in which they are working, and the way in which we carried out our research.

Sector representation

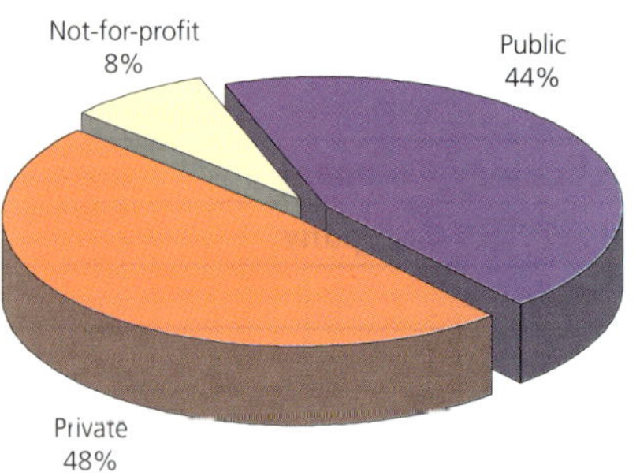

Figure 2

Figure 2 shows the population of interviewees analysed by sector. The women leaders came from a wide spread of organisations, as Figure 3 shows. Central Government was well represented (11 interviewees). Six interviewees came from retail organisations; and five came from each of non-departmental public bodies; professional services; not-for-profit; education; and media. Four women came from the health sector and four from information technology. Three came from the financial services sector and three from legal firms. There were two interviewees from each of the transport, telecoms, arts, local government, leisure, hotels & restaurants and distribution areas; and one each from pharmaceuticals, and oil and gas.

Industry representation

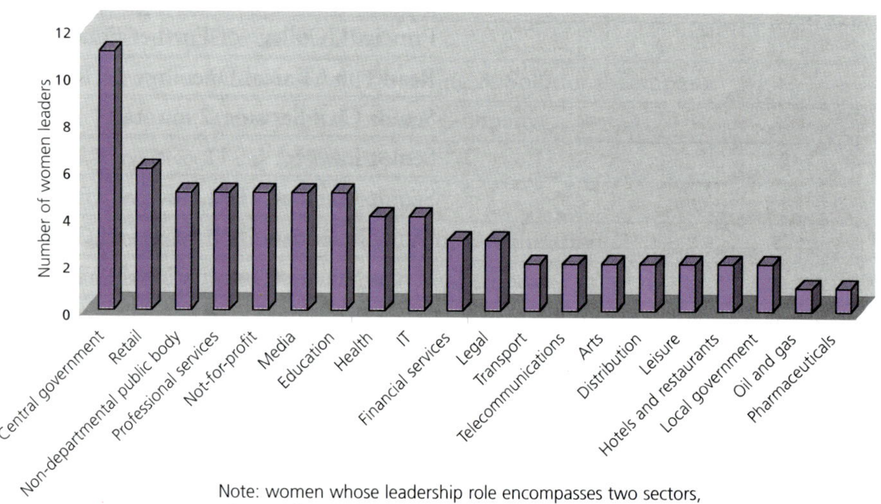

Note: women whose leadership role encompasses two sectors, such as professional services and I.T., have been allocated to both.

Figure 3

Leadership roles

Subsidiary board 8%

Middle management/ functional head 12%

Main board 80%

Top role 63%

Figure 4

Analysis of women leaders by role (Figure 4) shows that 80% of those interviewed are on the Main Board of their organisation. 63% also hold the "top role". That is, they are Chair, Chief Executive, Managing Director or Permanent Secretary (or equivalent) in their organisation. They are women who have "made it".

Figure 5 shows leadership role in relation to organisation size. It indicates that this research focuses upon women at more senior levels than previous research *(1)*.

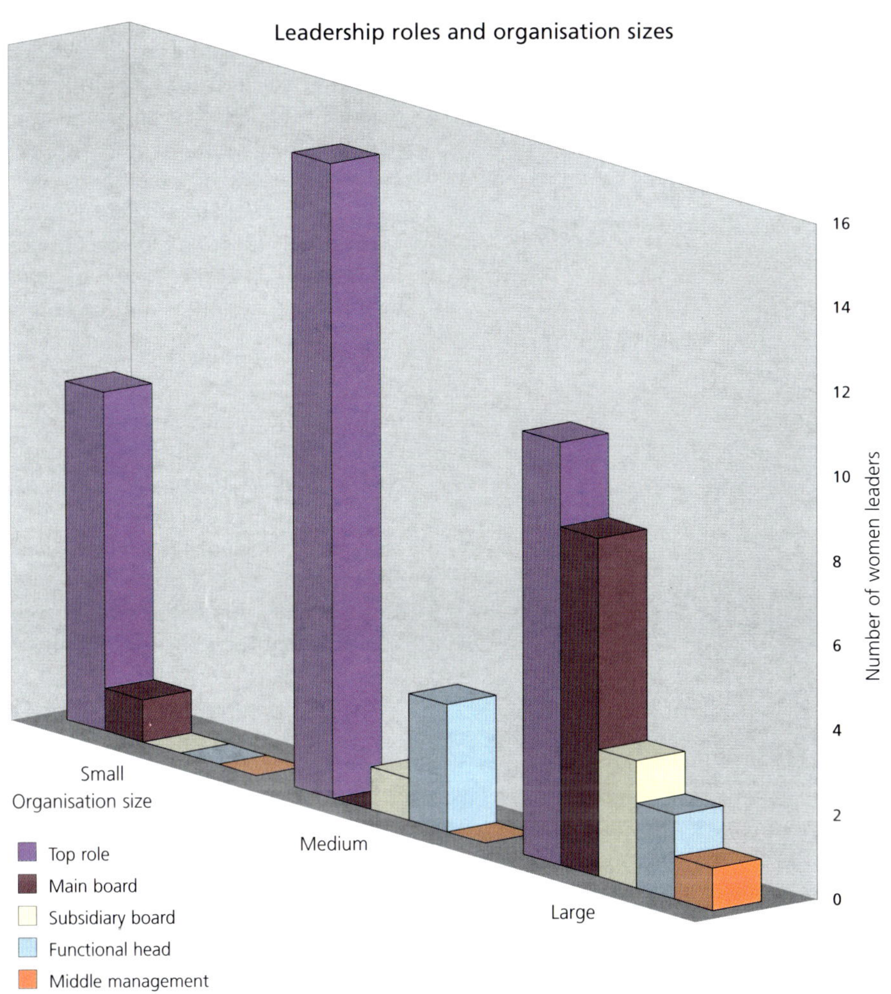

Figure 5

Carrying out the research

The stimulus for the work was the interest of both our organisations in leadership. More particularly, the focus for the three authors of this research is women's leadership: partly because we are all women, and partly because many of our clients are senior women. We wanted to understand something of the experience of a wide range of women in leadership roles in public and private sector organisations in the UK, in order the better to help our clients.

We wanted to explore their experience in depth, since as far as we could establish, this had not been done before in the UK. We therefore chose to interview a relatively small number of senior women (52) face-to-face, in depth, using a semi-structured framework (see Appendix II). The method we adopted was one of a qualitative open-ended exploration without an initial hypothesis. We were thus open to the full richness of our interviewees' experience. This is important, because anything that touches upon behavioural difference between men and women is potentially contentious. A detailed description of our method appears in Appendix I.

Our research population was a somewhat fortuitous assemblage, not a structured sample but a group of senior women whom we invited to take part in our study. Although the research is not representative, we made every effort to achieve a spread of industry sectors, and to include women in the public, private, and not-for-profit sectors, and in government. This has enabled us to tap into a variety of experiences of leadership, which is critically important because so much of leadership is determined by organisational context. Each woman took part in a 90-minute research interview with one of the three authors, and what each said was recorded verbatim. It is these interview accounts that form the basis of the findings reported here.

What the research is – and what it is not

We do not claim that the findings of this study are representative of all women leaders, and we do not draw any generic conclusions about women in general from the findings. It is important to note that this research does not map the experience of younger women, the women leaders of the future, or indeed of men.

Some studies have interviewed women at work, but they have not done so recently, nor have they focused, as this study does, on women at the top. Other studies have also been conducted by means of surveys or questionnaires, rather than by in-depth interviews, thus potentially limiting their richness *(2)*.

What this research does is to map the experience of these particular women leaders. It is an honest and compelling account of what we were told, in many hours of interviews, by fifty-two women in very senior positions in UK organisations at the end of the twentieth century.

In the next chapter, we turn to the women's stories, and let their voices speak for themselves.

References: Chapter 2

(1) A substantive study of "high flyer" women was published in 1992 which examined, inter alia, whether a separate theory of women's career development was needed. The researchers interviewed forty-eight women "who had achieved extraordinary levels of career success". See Barbara White, Charles Cox and Cary Cooper (1992) Women's Career Development: A Study of High Flyers: *Blackwell, Oxford.*

(2) See for example "The Women Who Move Britain" Kirstie Hamilton, Management Today *pp 39-46, March 1999*

Chapter 3

The changing culture of leadership

- Skills, qualities and attributes
- Leadership style and values
- Leaders of the future

As we heard our 52 women leaders speak about how they lead their organisations, we were struck by the sense that they had something new to say about leadership. Despite the diversity of sectors, industries and roles represented by the women we interviewed, their comments on what they bring to leadership in terms of skills, qualities and attributes are remarkably consistent; as are their opinions of what leadership in today's organisations is about; and their vision of leadership in the future. The crucial fact that is revealed by their comments is that women leaders have – for years – been leading in the way that management thinkers are now saying organisations should be led in the twenty-first century. In remaining true to themselves, these women have demonstrated leadership practices that are way ahead of their time.

3 The changing culture of leadership

Skills, qualities and attributes

Delivering on "the people and the numbers"

"I try to understand what goes on in people's hearts and minds and what is important to them and then match this to the goals of the organisation. These can work together in a well-functioning company and, if we can link them, it is a winning formula."

Managing Director, Global Information Technology Company

The positions these women have attained attest to their commercial and business acumen, but the most important finding about them is that they perceive themselves to be effective leaders both from the point of view of achieving the organisational task, whatever it might be, and in terms of looking after the people who do it with them or for them. They display a powerful combination of excellence at both "people and numbers". This is how one of our interviewees put it:

"I am very hardworking and I will get things done, even if that means staying up all night. People know that they can rely upon me. I am not political. I get on well with my clients which means I can develop business with them. I keep my ears open and I don't just develop business for my area but for other areas too. So it is not just the soft stuff! I can actually bring money in as well."

Board Member, International Professional Services Firm

Building committed and loyal teams

"I get a great sense of pleasure if somebody I have encouraged achieves something they thought they couldn't achieve."

Managing Director, International Retail Company

Many women spoke of their passion for and skill in building loyal teams. They believe that building emotional commitment into teams increases their strength and efficiency, as is illustrated in the preceding quote. Often, when women move companies, or start up on their own, they take these strong and loyal teams with them.

Being modest

"I am not bad at projecting ideas. I am not a bad advocate. I'm quite good at working with people. I'm persuasive rather than commanding."

Chair, Non-Departmental Public Body

Asked what skills they have as leaders, many women answered by telling us what they were not good at! This quality of playing down achievements has sometimes held women back, but in some cases, their declared weaknesses were merely the downside to their positive qualities:

"There was a phase when I gave too much power away; then I had to reclaim the authority. It was hard taking some power back."

Managing Director, Financial Services Firm

This willingness to face up to weaknesses and work at them is also an aspect of their enthusiasm for continued learning and intellectual challenge in their work.

Not playing politics

"I have an antipathy about getting into a more political role, where it is difficult to complete pieces of work. I don't like the idea of politically manoeuvring to achieve something."

Partner, Global Professional Services Firm

Many women said they disliked 'playing politics' and also did not feel it was a priority for them, perhaps because they are more skilled than some male colleagues at influencing others and creating collaboration without the use of divisive "game-playing".

"We don't want to spend time positioning we don't want to spend time manoeuvring all the time. Men are more 'strategic' – they position themselves on projects to help themselves move up the ladder".

Director, Multinational Media Company

Deploying their personal qualities and attributes as professional skills

"What are my skills? Inspiring loyalty, living values, being human. It works!"

Director, Multinational Information Technology Company

A striking finding is that who the women are as people defines them as leaders, so that the picture is one of them deploying their personal qualities and attributes as leadership skills. Rather than possessing an impersonal skill

Living their values

"I will not do everything just for money or success ... I owe it to myself and others not to lose sight of my values."

Managing Director, International Retailer

These women place a great deal of emphasis on clear, open leadership where people lead and develop their people by example, according to a strong set of personal values. The key elements of living their values are practicality, openness, flexibility and treating others with respect:

"I'm hugely practical and organised. People find me a good leader because I am very clear about where we are going and what we need to stand for, but not too prescriptive about how to get there. I think I'm quite good at seeing the whole. I don't get bogged down in my bit. I draw my ideas from my whole life."

Main Board Director, FTSE 100 Company

WHO SAID 'PUT HER AT THE BACK, SHE'LL BE OUT OF THE WAY' —?

"I have a particular style, which is open. My relationship with subordinates is one of respect. I don't pretend to be 'the expert' at anything. It is my job to create the strategy, to set the framework, the values, the behaviours for this division. Then I am the facilitator. I need to give them the things they need to get on with it. I have always found that people exceed my expectations, but you need to religiously reinforce the values. My subordinates feel they can say anything to me. I ask for upward feedback every year. Sometimes, I find pockets of behaviour which does not fit with my values. I have zero tolerance for behaviours that hit my hot buttons. I am clear about what I expect from people and this seems to go down really well because there is nothing worse than a lack of clarity about what is expected from you."

Board Director, FTSE 100 Company

Promoting autonomy and creativity

"I like to see people have their work recognised."

Managing Director, British Retail Company

In line with their passion for developing people and their ability to create effective teams, these women emphasise their roles as leaders in facilitating creativity in others:

"My people expect me to inspire them. A 'trusty' said to me "We need you to make the hair on the backs of our necks prickle". So I try now to say the unexpected!"

Senior Civil Servant

“Relationships in my firm are friendly. It is a flat organisation and completely female. In the leadership, we value motivation, innovative ideas, energy, intuition and initiative. Everybody has a second job within the company to develop her abilities. I deal these out according to their strengths.”

Managing Director, British Retail Company

The women demonstrate a tendency to stand back and allow others to shine. They see themselves not only as leaders, but also as facilitators, and they enjoy the caring and nurturing aspect of their work. These women describe “creative leadership which meets the bottom line”, a mixture of masculine and feminine qualities that makes things happen in organisations. The following quote is a wonderful example of this kind of leadership in action:

“There was a major disturbance on the wing, with 50 men out of their cells, up in arms about what they thought was poor quality food. I knew I had to do something or we could have a riot. I checked the kitchen – there was nothing else. All the staff and prisoners were looking to me. What I decided to do was to order 100 or so McDonalds’ Happy Meals. I took delivery of them myself and took every single one personally to each prisoner. It was an important moment. Life in prisons can be wrecked over food. It was crucial that I carried the prison officers with me and the prisoners were happy, as they felt they had been heard.”

Assistant Director, Civil Service

This woman leader successfully brought together her feminine skills of nurturing and personally caring for people together with the masculine skills of decision-making and risk-taking in a potentially dangerous situation. Another of our interviewees more closely defines this kind of leadership:

“I’m strong underneath but I have learned to be delicate. There is a North American Indian saying, which goes, ’He who is tough inside and soft outside is healer. He who is hard on the outside and soft inside is useless!’ A tough, hard, macho management style is no good. If you have no tenderness in you, you can’t do it. And if you are soft or weak inside, you can’t do it either. True strength is delicate.”

Principal, College of Further Education

This is emotional intelligence in practice *(2)*. It is also what others have called “transformational leadership” *(3)*. The transformation of the situation in the prison is a clear example of this. The need for transformation in organisations to sustain competitive advantage also requires this combination of qualities. In the next section, we will see how closely this aligns with the ideas of contemporary management thinkers about the style of leadership needed by organisations in the future. It perhaps represents the beginning of the drift to a new paradigm for the next generation of leadership.

Leaders of the future

"Principled, strong, dynamic, visible, living and breathing values."

Senior Civil Servant

Our 52 women leaders had firm ideas on the kind of leadership required by successful organisations in the future. Significantly, what they say about future needs is very like what they say about their leadership today – a refreshingly novel finding! Some representative quotes:

"Visionary leadership is important. You must aim high, reinventing ideas and representing them appropriately. You must set out your personal values as well as your organisational values, so that you can raise your personal sights as well as the organisation's sights. You need empathy and lots of emotional quotient in order to understand what makes workforces tick."

Chair, Non-Departmental Public Body

"You need to be charismatic, flexible and create a culture where people feel valued."

Director, Multinational Media Company

"It [the culture] is going to be very practical, open, flatter, more strategic at senior levels, customer-focused and still maintaining high standards."

Main Board Director, FTSE 100 Company

"We need an emergent leadership style, where you are able to develop things 'in the moment' of the organisation at all levels. I am an advocate of leadership blossoming everywhere. We need to give the space for leadership ability to develop in everyone."

Director, Professional Services Firm

"We are trying to create a culture that does not rely upon command and control but one where people's creativity is encouraged. However, it is tough to manage from the middle, not from the front. Instead of being the one who shows people how to do everything, you guide from the middle, supporting people to know that they can make something happen which is in line with your goals.”

Board Director, FTSE 100 Company

“Leadership involves the 3 ‘V’s: values, vision and voice. All involve working with people. Leadership is about setting people free! This requires congruence between the rest of one’s life and one’s values.”

Chair, Non-Departmental Public Body

These women are already practising the kind of leadership that they define as the leadership of the future. What do management thinkers have to say about this?

A major challenge for organisations is said to be the need to achieve business transformation ahead of the next wave of turbulence in their world *(4)*. To win, they will need more and better information, insight and intelligence at all levels, and to allow people at all levels the space to make good decisions, because only in that way will organisations cope with conditions of ever greater uncertainty. Put another way, decision-making will need to be more instantaneous than before, closer to the point of contact with the consumer, and better tailored to suit the particular needs of the customer or client. The impact of e-learning and e-commerce is still not fully understood. This implies far more time and attention needs to be spent on developing employees to understand the business as a whole and to help them to carry on lifelong learning. All employees will need to become more involved in the business both in terms of input (creative thinking and ideas, and handling feedback direct from the clients/customers) and output (the effective delivery of precisely targeted products or services) *(5)*.

If this description of organisations of the future is accurate, and there is a growing body of evidence to suggest that this is so, then the command and control systems built over many years in established organisations will no longer be optimal. Leadership and management will need to be quite differently focused – less about control and more about influence, less about management and more about leadership. This means inspiring and influencing people to follow and it seems likely they will follow more willingly where they have had a hand in helping to create their own environment. This implies a rather different blend of skills and intelligence for successful leadership in the future.

Intuition (in the sense of using 'emotional intelligence' alongside rigorous analysis) clearly has its place here, along with negotiated authority, which is acceptable to and acknowledged by both leader and led *(6)*. This means collaboration becomes an important skill, as does having the courage to present oneself as a human being to one's colleagues, warts and all. The 'glue' that integrates the organisation will be of a different kind *(7)*. In theory, this might mean making oneself more vulnerable, by becoming more transparent and accessible, the prize being the building of an enduring mutual trust and support *(8)*.

This model is richer than Goleman's *(9)* E.Q. (or emotional intelligence) thesis, according to Mant *(10)* because it involves 'broad band intelligence' beyond mere personal skills. Taffinder *(11)* emphasises the importance of being able to 'impose context' or the idea of winning lasting commitment to a vision and a concomitant strategy. While this implies the ability to be tough, and deal with conflict, Mant says it also involves an understanding of how change in one part of the organisation or its competitive environment will produce 'ripples' elsewhere which need to be anticipated and managed. It also involves the capacity for timely judgement.

The fact that existing command and control style organisation structures are changing (in the ways outlined above) potentially gives women more of a chance to enter the field, in the sense that those models may be seen as patriarchal (and thus male-dominated) structures, which women have hitherto found hard to enter at very senior levels *(12)*.

The depth of skills women inherently seem to display in facilitation, collaboration and people development, combined with their commitment to learning *(13)*, will serve them well in the dispersed, flatter customer-focused organisation structures of the future. This should also help in the creation of people development strategies for women and men that fit better with turn-of-the-century aspirations.

Since women have clearly articulated sets of principles and values that guide them at work, this also fits with the idea of 'principle-centred leadership' espoused by Stephen Covey *(14)* and the 'conviction' mentioned by Paul Taffinder *(15)* at the centre of his leadership model of the future.

Although there has been some rhetoric on these themes, for instance that 'the future is female', there is also a view that the harder-edged skills, such as 'risk-making and risk-taking' *(15a)* may not come so easily to women, and some of our women executives alluded to this. The ability to manage in uncertain (and hence higher-risk) situations, and the ability to deal with and use aggression as needed to push through organisational change are less naturally associated with women *(16)*. These skills may need to be learned by women, just as men must learn the people skills to which women appear to have easier access. It is also likely to be true that good male leaders use this blend of skills that the 52 women here talk about, blending what have traditionally been seen as masculine or feminine skills is eminently practicable. In fact this is by no means a difficult process though it may be prudent to give greater emphasis to the 'harder competencies', the better to develop women executives with all round skills.

It is clear that at least some of our 52 women, by their own account, have already developed this new kind of leadership, which blends masculine and feminine skills in a balanced way. We discovered a remarkable consistency between the self reports of the 52 women leaders':

- skills, qualities and attributes
- leadership style and values
- views on leaders of the future
- views of new organisation forms coming into existence
- key writing on leadership for organisations of the future.

We feel it is right to see this as changing the culture of leadership and marking the way for the majority of men and women to follow.

References: Chapter 3

(1) Kabacoff, R and Peters, H (1999) Leadership and Gender: a Comparison of Leadership Style, *Management Research Group Paper*

(2) Goleman, D (1998) Working with Emotional Intelligence *Bantam Books, New York*

(3) Rosner, J (1990) "Ways women lead". Harvard Business Review *November – December 1990*

(4) Taffinder, P (1995) The New Leaders: Achieving Corporate Transformation Through Dynamic Leadership *Kogan Page; London*

(5) Hirschhorn, L (1997) Re-Working Authority: Leading and Following in the Post-Modern Organisation *MIT Press; Cambridge, Mass*

(6) Mant, A (1997) Intelligent Leadership *Allen & Unwin, St Leonard's, New South Wales*

(7) Covey, S (1992) Principle-Centered Leadership *Simon and Schuster; London*

(8) Hirschhorn, L (1997) Ibid

(9) Goleman, D (1998) Ibid

(10) Mant, A (1997) Ibid

(11) Taffinder, P (1995) Ibid

(12) Nicolson, P (1996) Gender, Power and Organisation; A Psychological Perspective *Routledge; London*

(13) Baker-Miller, J (1986) The New Psychology of Women *Beacon Press, Boston, MA*

(14) Covey, S (1992) Ibid

(15) Taffinder, P (1995) Ibid

(15a) Ibid

(16) Halton, W (1999) Personal communication

My baby's worth more than my £¼m salary

Mother love – it's the real thing

Women still face uphill trek to place on board

Women fight for pension rights

Women put pressure on the glass ceiling

The number of female executives may be rising, but their progress to the boardroom is still slow, the survey shows

Why women make better managers

'I felt so mistreated by male colleagues that I just had to resign'

Dixons recruits 'superwoman'

Bye-bye baby, I'm off to work again

Extending the shelf life of women

Women on course for top posts in management

Chapter 4

How the women lead: some contributory factors

- Family background
- Education
- Drivers
- Career management

In this chapter, we investigate some of the reasons why our 52 women leaders lead in the way that they do – in the way we see as changing the culture of leadership. The strand we explore here is the individual case histories of these women – the life experience and internal factors, such as motivation – which have led to their success and their particular style of good leadership. In Chapter 5, we will look at another related strand, that of external influences on their career, and their leadership style.

4 How the women lead: some contributory factors

Family background

Birth order

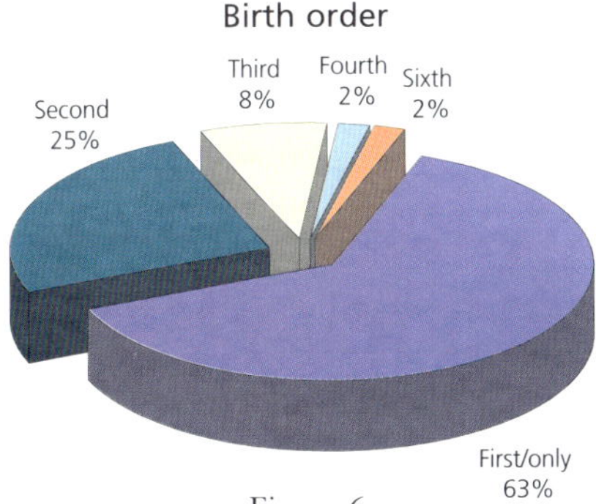

Figure 6

"I am the older sister – so can be bossy and like being in control."

Head of Function, NHS

As can be seen from the rather startling Figure (6), 63% of women were the only child, or oldest sibling in the birth order. This finding is significant at the p<.001 level. Even if one takes into account that family sizes in the UK tend to be small (so the chances of being a third, fourth or fifth child are dramatically lower than being a first or second born) these findings are still highly significant. They are in line with previous findings that women and men, in leadership roles, tend to be the only or oldest children in the family *(1)*. One suggested explanation of this finding is that, if you are an only or oldest child, you have more direct experience than younger siblings of the parental leadership of the family "organisation", from which children learn by role modelling.

"I am the eldest, number 1, and I have got this thing about being the best I can be."

Chief Executive, Not-for-Profit organisation

Clearly, there could be implications for children born later in the birth order about the need to deal with what could be seen in achieving a leadership role – as an inbuilt disadvantage of birth. But in that context it is interesting to note that most of the newcomers to 'Fortune' magazine's recent list of "The 50 Most Powerful Women" (in US business) were youngest or middle order children in birth order. To quote Patricia Sellers, writing in "Fortune" about this list, "Experts say that later borns tend to be pioneers and innovators." *(2)*

Family view of education

"It was a very goal-orientated environment."

Managing Director, International Retailer

Many women spoke of the importance of family encouragement of achievement at school which they link directly to their professional success:

"I was influenced by my family's valuing of education. It was important to do well at school. I was the first person in my extended family to go to university."

Executive Manager, Global Telecommunications Company

"In my family, there was a big emphasis on education. There were no constraints put on us by my family about what we could do."

Chair, Non-Departmental Public Body

"I was an only child, encouraged by both parents to develop to my full ability."

Managing Director, International Retailer

Support and Encouragement from the Family

"I had amazingly 'allowing' but interested parents."

Partner, Global Professional Services Firm

Most women spoke warmly of the support and encouragement given to them by their parents, not only in terms of education but also in terms of building confidence, self-belief and high aspirations; and creating a family environment of "achievement orientation".

"My parents encouraged me in whatever I wished to do throughout my childhood. I now realise how rare this is in parents. Mine did not push any of their expectations onto me or my brother. I bumped up against this with the contrast at Cambridge with other students managing their parents' expectations."

Partner, Global Professional Services Firm

"There is a belief that stemmed from my parents that I am capable; a feeling of confidence and worth that I had something to contribute. When you are working in a change agent role, you have to rely on yourself in the beginning and so this early support from my parents has been vital."

Chair, Non-Departmental Public Body

"People who are good leaders are secure in themselves and if they are not, they use the job wrongly, to bolster themselves personally. You have to inculcate a sense of security, identity and who you are in your early upbringing. You can't put it there if it does not exist."

Chair, Non-Departmental Public Body

Despite the fact that many of the women's mothers did not have professional careers they helped shape their daughters' early career development:

"There's no doubt that my mother had a huge influence on my career. My sister was the first in the family to go to university. I was number two! My mother left school at the age of 14. My sister and I had to stand on our own two feet, pushed by our mother. There was a lot less pressure on my brother. My mother was determined the two girls would never have to be dependent on anyone. There was a lot of push but never unkindly. There was the feeling that we should never depend on anyone financially."

Board Member, International Professional Services Firm

Other women were particularly encouraged by their fathers and some by other male relatives, such as an uncle or much older brother. A few women spoke of having parents who did not provide much encouragement, and of the damaging effects of this lack of support on their self confidence.

"I didn't apply to Oxbridge although my teachers wanted me to. If my parents had understood the significance, they might have encouraged me. They were puzzled and bemused and did not believe in reward for achievement like some of my friends' parents did. The attitude was 'God gave you a brain, so use it and it's your hard luck if you don't!'"

Assistant Director, Civil Service

Two women spoke of the effects of their mothers' frustrated career ambitions. One said:

"My mother was very bright, intelligent and frustrated. She lived vicariously through her daughters and always wanted me to succeed professionally. I felt the need to do well, compensating for her inability to have a job. She took a lot of pride in educating us but was very unconfident herself, not a happy person. I have an amazing memory of myself aged 5 with a round ballet bag leaving home. Everything I have done since then is about being an individual, wanting to be true to myself and leave the confines of my claustrophobic family. My mother said, 'You can't always do the things in life you want to do' and I thought 'Why not?'"

Deputy Chair, International Arts Organisation

Influence of the Family on Career Choices

"My career choice was affected by my family background but I didn't realise it at the time."

Principal, College of Further Education

Career similarites with their parents

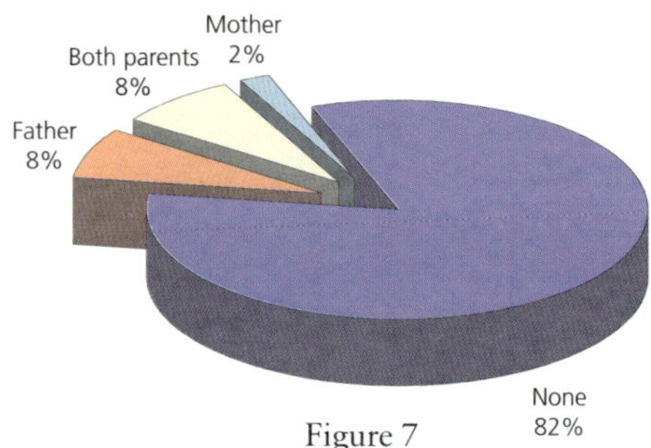

Figure 7

As can be seen from Figure 7, very few women have followed careers in the same or even similar areas to their mother or father. A few women mentioned a direct influence of their family on their career choices. Here is an example:

"My grandfather was a big influence. He was from Russia. My ex-husband bought me a rabbit coat for £13. He was very proud. My grandfather said 'From this she gets a disease!' My father was a master tailor. Off-cuts made little clothes for me ... I have an absolute love for clothes, a passion for it! From the age of 6 or 8 I was felling hems. I was in the workroom and I watched my father."

Managing Director, Retail Company

This woman went on to become a leading fashion retailer. For most women, however, the influences were more subtle: they picked up on a general sense of values which has been carried through into career choices:

"My grandfather was a brilliant vicar in the Welsh valleys. He knew everyone and their families and connections. Across the world that I work in I do well in remembering people. I remember their career details. People love to talk about themselves and remembering what matters to people and connecting it on is a great skill. That rather female trait, maybe a Welsh trait, has helped me in this world. People call it networking now!"

Chief Executive, Not-for-Profit Organisation

"My career choice was affected by my family background but I didn't realise it at the time. My unconscious experience of mother and father working together in a family business, totally devoted to high quality. You don't survive if you don't give customer satisfaction."

Principal, College of Further Education

Mothers working outside home

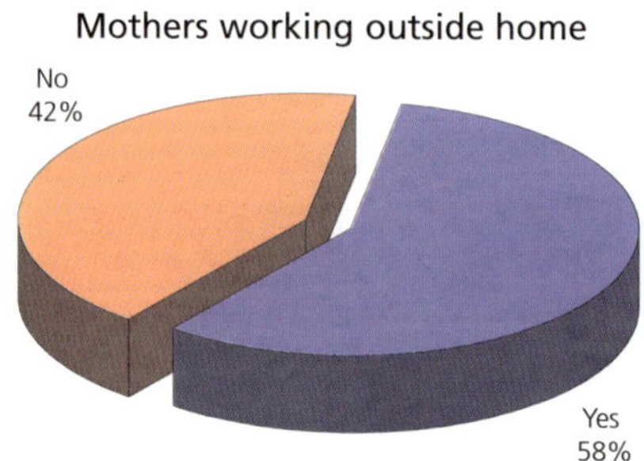

Figure 8

Even though 82% of the women do not have careers which are similar to those of either of their parents, something they share with the majority of men. We were interested to find out how many of the women had mothers who worked outside the home. The figure illustrates our findings. 58% of the women had mothers who worked outside the home, which was not common in the UK prior to the 1960s. This may have given them role models for managing their later work and home lives as adults.

The unifying theme in the women's comments on their family background was of the importance of family support in engendering the self-confidence that is vital to being a successful leader. Whilst there is nothing apparently gender-specific in the need for prospective leaders to have encouragement and support in their family backgrounds, perhaps the stress the women place on it is because of some of the difficulties they have faced in getting to the top, simply on account of their gender. So they feel self-confidence is important to carry them through. This has clear implications for parents who wish to support their children's, especially their daughters', achievements.

The birth order finding is important for parents and developers of leaders alike in that children born later in the birth order may have deeply held expectations about leadership derived from early childhood experience – for example that someone else will do it! Parents and coaches of potential leaders who are later born will need to help these people work at exploring such potentially limiting personal expectations of achievement.

Education

Most of the women leaders attached great significance to the quality of their education, especially those who were late starters at higher education for reasons of a disadvantaged childhood or poor progress at ordinary school. Not all the women have higher education, but the group has an impressive battery of qualifications, as can be seen in Figure 9.

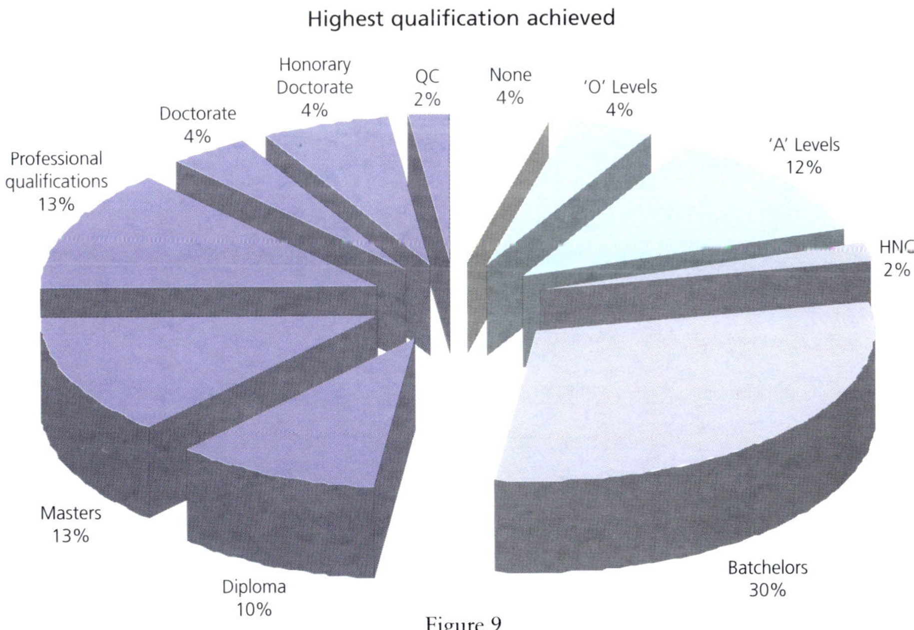

Figure 9

All girls' schools

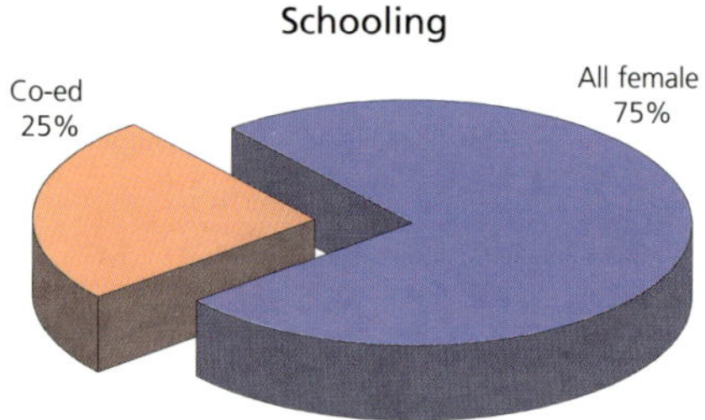

Figure 10

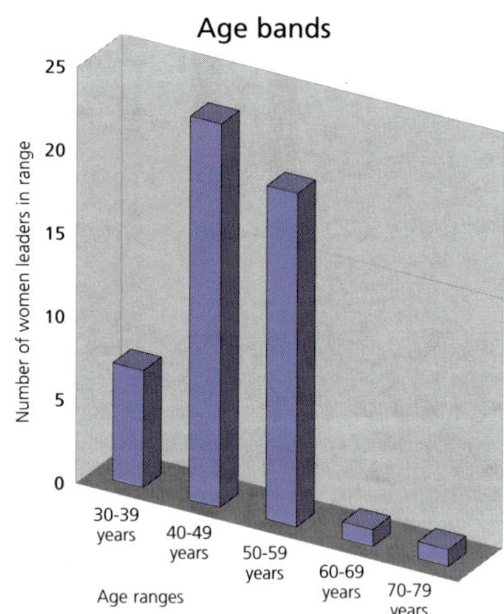

Figure 11

"At least at a girls' grammar school, I saw the woman I could become. It seemed attainable and understandable."

Principal, College of Further Education

It is highly significant that most of these successful women attended all girls' schools, even if one takes into account that choice of school was limited: this is because the availability of all girls' schooling through the state system has fluctuated in Britain. The majority of our women are in their 40's and 50's (see Figure 11) and would have had access to more single sex education than those born later. In the 60's, there were some state single sex schools, but by the 70's, most of them had gone, swept away by the move towards comprehensive schools, which were usually mixed. Throughout this century, single sex options were abundant across the independent schooling sector. This single sex option in the independent sector has grown slightly since state schools became comprehensive. The women in this sample appear evenly distributed in their attendance at state and independent schools. Many of them said that attending an all girls' school was important to them.

"At a girls' school, women can take on all the roles and that helped because you did not have to give in to men."

Principal, College of Further Education

"Going to a girls' school was a great benefit because there is no peer pressure. You don't get the boffin label which can be quite cruel. You don't have to worry that your lipstick is on straight!"

Senior Scientist, International Pharmaceuticals Company

Whilst the current trend in state education in the UK is for comprehensive schools, this research adds support to the argument that all girls' schooling is better than mixed schooling for encouraging women's achievement in the workplace.

The quality of encouragement

"Individual teachers took an interest in me and made me feel special."

Chair, Non-Departmental Public Body

Whichever kind of school attended, a number of women talked about the encouragement and support given to them by teachers, for example:

"School taught me to achieve well and encouraged me. It was a very good education and there was no question that you could not achieve things as a woman."

Senior Lawyer

Some women were more critical and said their schools had actually limited their ambition by suggesting jobs with few prospects of advancement. Here is one woman with an interesting twist in her story:

"Being a non-Catholic at a Catholic convent school was the beginning of it all. Discovering that you can be presented with givens in life which you do not have to accept (for example, the Pope is not infallible) and that you can even change. If I map my career, I became an accountant because the careers office at university told me that being an accountant was not a career for a woman. The Pope has a lot to answer for! He is responsible for all this!"

Managing Director, Executive Search Firm

The influence of peers

"There were lots of very interesting girls together in the same school."

Chief Executive, International Not-for-Profit Organisation

It is clear that these women were also inspired by the achievements of their peers at school, some of whom are still part of a close network today.

Drivers

We were particularly interested in interviewing these women to discover what motivates them, day to day.

Caring for people

"I love seeing people succeed, grow and take things on."

Chair, Non-Departmental Public Body

This theme had a number of elements. The first and most frequently mentioned was a passion for developing others, and huge satisfaction in seeing others achieve:

"I get a great sense of pleasure if somebody I have encouraged achieves something they thought they couldn't achieve. It takes them one rung up and I always get pleasure from that."

Chief Executive, Educational Institution

“I have a strong motivation to help people and I want people to be working and loving what they do. I deflect the accolade to other people and try to bring out the best in them and help them go for gold.”

Chief Executive, National Not-for-Profit Organisation

Within this theme of developing people there appears to be a strong flavour of a need to nurture people, to make them feel good about themselves. Some women explicitly relate this to the use of familial feelings at work.

“The model I use instinctively is the family model. I learned from how I brought up my children. The organisation hierarchy is a bit like a family. The task is to get people to take on responsibility without first abandoning them. You must give people the feeling both parties are learning or it's too persecutory. In relationships with adults, you should not use power to get what you want. There should be sufficient authority to influence people to work in a way which will result in learning happening.”

Executive Director, National Arts Organisation

Many women talked about the importance of having a cause or social ideals, a strong sense of values, and this perhaps to an extent reflects the number of women in our sample from the public or not-for-profit sector, although women from a variety of organisational settings talked about social ideals as a driver:

“A personal sense of value drives me. In a way it relates to integrity. I will not do anything just for money or success. My life is a trade-off all the time between running a four minute mile because I am driven, and wanting to smell the flowers along the way. I owe it to myself and others not to lose sight of my values. However badly people behave, I try to ignore things and keep focused on the good of the business. At the end of the day, to be dishonest or fraudulent, I feel there would be personal damage to me. So a culture which is honest and striving for integrity – I feel more comfortable in it.”

Managing Director, International Retailer

Several women mentioned religious values and principles as a source of inspiration:

“I am a practising Christian and it has a big influence on me – trying to treat people how I want to be treated myself and being aware of others' feelings. When things are particularly difficult, I pray, asking for wisdom and trying to find the inner resources to deal with unpleasant situations.”

Senior Civil Servant

Many women mentioned their commitment to helping other women but often with the caveat that they were not feminists. They reported that they had to be helpful without shouting about it, for fear of attracting negative opinions (i.e. gaining a feminist tag) from male colleagues. The wish to help other women was given by some of our interviewees as one of the reasons for taking part in this research.

The quest for excellence and intellectual challenge

"I'm NOT just average!"

Director, Global Information Technology Company

This theme was also a very strong one and may reflect the wisdom that, if you are a woman, you have to be the best to succeed. It had several aspects. Firstly, our women spoke of seeking perfection and the highest standards for themselves, and sometimes in others too:

"It's all about being the best. Being at the cutting edge. And the second division doesn't count. You want to do it right. It's not about money or power or massaging egos. Women like to do a job well."

Reader in Clinical Oncology, NHS

"I'm incredibly conscientious and hate things not being good enough. A lot of men don't have the same standards. My job would be easier if others had the same high standards."

Assistant Director, Civil Service

"I'm cautious in new environments. I function over 100% to make sure I am ahead of everyone. This might be part of the inferiority feelings I once had at secondary school – I'm not going to let those feelings take me over! I'm NOT just average!"

Director, Global Information Technology Company

There is a strong flavour of 'can do' about these women. They like to produce results, and achieve difficult goals:

"I like outcomes. I'd find it hard to be in a job that has no outcomes. I set myself goals and I want to see them delivered. I think that's why my job satisfies me."

Chair, Non-Departmental Public Body

“I'm very goal-orientated. I always ask myself 'What am I trying to achieve?' I work backwards from my goal in the quickest most quality way and then start from there. I don't give up on things I believe in.”

Managing Director, Global Information Technology Company

Linked to the quest for excellence is the finding that some of the women are driven by a wish to gain praise, recognition or the approbation or even envy of others. Alternatively some are driven by wanting to avoid disapproval, or by fear of failure. This bears on the earlier point the women made about the importance of self confidence to leadership, but is probably not gender-specific *(3)*. Indeed it seems to demonstrate that in terms of goal-orientation there is no difference between men and women. The women in our sample drive themselves very hard and measure themselves against absolute standards, rather than against colleagues.

“I'm needing affirmation all the time. I've had more affirmation here than anywhere else. I get asked to do a lot here at work and in the community – 'Talent recognises genius and mediocrity sees only itself'. This climate does give affirmation and I am able to rise to the challenge.”

Principal, College of Further Education

“I am driven by low self-esteem and fear of failure. Having exceptionally high standards and goals, some of which came from my parents, absolute goals and a feeling that there was some duty to develop yourself and to be the best you could. Naively, I look to other people and role models and measure myself against an absolute model of compassion and intelligence, which is very tough.”

Managing Director, International Retailer

The streak of perfectionism and the desire for achievement is strongly linked to these women's need for intellectual challenge in their work.

“It was only worth doing because it is hard. You want to do the right thing and you want to do it well. There's research that needs doing. I was driven by a desire to make a difference. If you are going to work – and that means worries and missing the kids – it's got to be something important. There's also the academic drive. I do need to be academically satisfied as well. There's huge pleasure for that, using your brain.”

Reader in Clinical Oncology, NHS

Determination

"Coming second is not an option."

Chief Executive, International IT Staffing and Solutions Company

We found that these women are a dogged lot. In some ways, by definition, this has to be so in that they are the successful minority that has got to the top:

"Dogged determination! I can encapsulate it in my 6 'P's; Planning (and replanning and replanning); Preparing (getting yourself ready to be indispensable); Perspiration; Persistence (look upon obstacles as stepping stones); Passion (you must love what you do and passionately want what you want, doing the best job); Payback (latterly I have realised that I have become conscious how important it is to give back to people. Colleagues are more proactive then in helping you to succeed)."

Board Director, FTSE 100 Company

"I have always tried to do things I can't do! I join things when people are leaving and see opportunities when things look disastrous – in situations of change, crisis or big problems. You can then make a tremendous difference. For example, with one contract which was make or break. I was then managing people who were previously very senior to me, a den of lions! I had to be constantly ahead of the game, pushing out the envelope and finding the next piece of insecurity. It's because of my low boredom threshold and my desire to get peace inside."

Director, Multinational Information Technology Company

A number of women talked about significant life events that have shaped their careers. There were traumatic and difficult experiences in childhood, such as circumstances of extreme poverty and distressing family relationships, parental alcoholism, and early bereavement. As adults, some of them have had failed marriages, bankruptcy, sick children and personal experience of serious illness. But, far from derailing their careers, these women describe how events gave them new determination and focus, even giving them a reason to carry on and be successful. So, whereas lesser mortals might have given up in the face of adversity, it seems these women set great store on what one woman called the "alchemy of being able to turn the bad into good".

Not money in itself

"I am very independent minded. Financial independence is a main driver."

Managing Director, Global Information Technology Company

Our women are often strongly motivated by entrepreneurship, as this quote shows:

“Competing is incredibly important. I want this business to be the biggest and best in the field. The growth of the company to its limit drives me enormously.”

Managing Director, Global Information Technology Company

This motivation is however not primarily about money. Very few women mentioned money as a driver, and then it was more likely due to a wish for the independence money can bring, rather than a desire to be wealthy in itself. Here is a typical quote on this topic:

“My decisions have not been money-led but once I'm offered a job, I want to get the most I can out of it. I am the main breadwinner in the family. Money is important – there has to be enough of it. One of the things about my company is that they would support my family in case of catastrophe. But money has never been a main driver for me.”

Director, Multinational Media Company

These findings about the motivation of senior executive women are very much in line with previous much larger scale studies which also report others' evaluations of women leaders' actual leadership behaviour *(4)*. In other words, caring for people translates into a more democratic and participative leadership style, and the quest for excellence translates into high standards of performance and attainment of results, while determination translates into the greater energy, intensity and emotional expression observed in women in contrast to men.

Career Management

Unplanned career paths

“My career has not been planned. It has just happened!”

Chair, Non-Departmental Public Body

The striking thing about the career progress of these women is the number who describe it as unplanned and reactive to opportunities. Apart from two notable exceptions, 50 of the women describe their careers as if their career success was not 'serious', and just happened to them, rather than being planned in any way, or being the result of ambition or a grand vision:

I HAVEN'T PLANNED MY CAREER… I'M JUST LOOKING FOR CHALLENGES

"I've had no strategy at all! People have offered me jobs – zig-zagging progress and I've either taken them or not … The weird thing is that since doing this job, a whole load of other possibilities have opened up that I wasn't aware of would be attractive to me. And I suppose I've realised I'm quite good at it and it's only leading 200 people, but I can do it!"

Director, Multinational Media Company

"I have concentrated hugely on the job I was doing at one time. I was not looking out at the next job I wanted to do at all. I was always thirsty for the next challenge and felt that I could make a contribution. As a specialist, I wanted to be included in making decisions. I have rarely said "no" to opportunities, no matter how scary the new role was. People see you performing in things other than your main role."

Main Board Director, FTSE 100 Company

"I lack ambition but not drive. I'm not particularly bothered about status. In order to measure progress, you have to be able to monitor it from A to B to C. I haven't measured my career in that way. I tend to respond to things as they arise; there is no great element of planning. The bits in the rest of my life I spend more time worrying about."

Managing Director, Executive Search Firm

Seizing the Day

"You have to spot the lucky times and make the most of them!"

Senior Lawyer

It is clear that these women have been reactive to opportunities in their career development, seeing chances and taking them, however risky. Many of them mention luck as a factor although clearly serendipity works best for those clever and observant enough to spot opportunities:

"I've had good fortune and I'm very good at what I do, but there are better people. There is being in the right place at the right time. I know good people who work hard but don't get there. They don't have the luck I have had."

Director, Global Information Technology Company

"Mostly I've been plucked out of what I've been doing and pointed towards something else. As a successful person, you had the sense that something was coming up and you were considered to be in the field."

Former Director, Multinational Media Company

WE NEED SOMEONE WHO'S DETERMINED TO GET TO THE TOP

“It was a big career change to become a Senior Civil Servant. Someone suggested it. I would never have thought of it. It appealed because of the management element and because it was different from my previous experience. There has been a big combination of determination to succeed and maximising on lucky breaks.”

Senior Lawyer

Career choices led by the potential for learning

“I've been on a quest to understand things.”

Managing Director, Financial Services Company

These women's career choices have not been about hierarchy or status or power, but about other sources of satisfaction, primarily the potential for learning, which links to the driver of a need for intellectual challenge:

“I think one of the factors that has been significant is the desire to keep growing and doing different things. I am also unwilling to believe that things can't be fixed or sorted out. I've never found myself short of a challenge. I've always got more things I want to do, to fix. This has meant that I push out the boundaries of my job. I think a desire to bring people together makes things happen. It has never felt static. My jobs have always been growing and changing.”

Partner, City Law Firm

Given that these women are reactive to career opportunities rather than proactive in seeking them out, they are inevitably highly dependent on the organisational culture in which they find themselves, and the level of encouragement and support they get from their managers and colleagues. They have tended to be skilled in adapting themselves to their environments, but the lack of proactivity has often meant that they have had to wait for opportunities to present themselves, thus potentially slowing their career progress. There is also perhaps an implicit assumption built in to some of what they say that they have not been able to progress through traditional channels, possibly because the criteria for advancement are generally set to male standards, which do not easily fit them.

One of the key themes about the women's family background and education has been the emphasis on the need for support and encouragement to create self-confidence. Even though most of them were encouraged at home and at school, most of them were not confidently proactive in their career management. Why should this be?

It is perhaps related to a key driver, the quest for excellence, the felt need "to function at 150%" to ensure a position founded in certainty. Kram and McCollum *(5)* describe a 'visibility-vulnerability spiral' in which women in leadership operate under intense scrutiny and tend to be criticised more often, because they are in a minority. This conforms to the idea *(6)* that women derive more of their sense of identity and self-esteem from others, and thus criticism increases their internal sense of vulnerability. Our women feel this accounts for the fact that only highly competent women succeed – in other words, those who are less likely to be criticised for poor performance anyway. In support of this view, they referred to the desire to avoid criticism and failure and of their fear of being "found out" as "no good after all".

There is another basic viewpoint. Leiberman *(7)* describes how men use conflict and express anger in the workplace more easily than women. Men tend to feel highly uncomfortable about expressing any lack of confidence at work as it may make them seem not just less competent, but less masculine. They may just possibly project their lack of confidence onto women who are in the minority in the workplace. Women, in their desire to fit into the organisation, may then find themselves absorbing the general doubts, uncertainties and emotions in work that others, men, disown. They may therefore find themselves speaking up on issues about which others – their male colleagues – remain silent. As a result, women may be valued for their different perspective but may also be perceived as 'not being able to take the pressure', 'being too emotional', and insufficiently confident. Thus the potential for the erosion of their own self-confidence is exacerbated by carrying uncertainties and baggage belonging to others, increasing feelings of vulnerability and stress, which may in extremes lead women to leave the organisation. Other women, though not our 52 women as far as we (or they!) could tell, may respond to this dilemma by adopting some of the more extreme male behaviours, aping aggressive styles of leadership, perhaps in order not to attract criticisms associated with their femininity/assumed vulnerability.

If one discounts for a moment the powerful effect of organisational cultures in determining people's behaviour (and this will be examined in some depth in Chapter 6) and also the confidence issue that has been examined above, what might be going on below the surface in the women's minds to influence their approach to the workplace? Freud *(8)* would say that it stems from early childhood and the very different ways in which boys and girls are brought up, shaping their attitudes and expectations of life ever afterwards. In his view, boys' masculinity is defined by becoming separate from their mothers and 'the feminine world', by playing boys' games, and being encouraged to be active, interpersonally competitive and rough in play from early on in life. This has usually been perceived as preparing boys for the power games and politics of organisational life. Girls' femininity is seen as being defined by continuing attachment to their mothers. Their chosen activities and play are more concerned with preserving and equalising relationships with others – girls are taught to temper what they say so as not to sound too aggressive or certain. Standing out from the crowd is not approved of for girls *(9)*. Girls are thus said to have a difficulty becoming 'separate' in adolescence, preoccupied as they are with connection with others *(10)*. This leads to more difficulty competing with others and dealing with conflict and aggression in organisations.

However, as we have seen in Chapter 3, women's natural leadership style of collaboration and building commitment in teams, which derives from their upbringing, may be seen as a strength, not a weakness and represents the way forward for leadership of the future. As we have suggested, women are doing now what management thinkers say all leaders should do in the future. What the women say about their career management may reflect the time lag between their leadership style, the recognition that this is what organisations actually need, and then the will and capacity to create the changes to make it happen. In the meantime, some women may become frustrated at their inability to set the agenda. Their only escape might be to set up their own businesses, which some of the women in this research have done, running them in rather different ways to their male counterparts. It is significant that in the US, at least, more small business starts are made by women than by men.

The concern might be that change is still happening too slowly for women who do not wish merely to 'fit in' to pre-existing career paths or wait for things to happen. There is much to suggest that many men also feel uncomfortable with the existing order. Frosh *(11)* suggests that men are condemned by the anxiety that they can never match up to the expectation of their power, especially in relation to other men. Men may feel just as lacking in self-confidence as women, and may also be willing to express this for themselves, not through women.

There are also early signs of the changes in the psychological contract between organisations and their employees. Neither men nor women wish to be pushed into stereotypical roles associated with their gender any more. Increasingly, the wish and need seems to be for people to be able to bring more of themselves to work, vulnerabilities and all. This can only benefit men and women alike.

References: Chapter 4

(1) White B, Cox C, and Cooper C (1992) Women's Career Development: A Study of High Flyers *Blackwell Business, Oxford*

(2) Sellers, P. (1999) "The Fifty Most Powerful Women" *Fortune no.20, October 25 1999*

(3) Although, in their comparison of men's and women's leadership style, Kabacoff and Peters report that women are far more focused on high standards and excellence in performance than men. See Kabacoff, R and Peters, H (1999) Leadership and Gender: A Comparison of Leadership Style Between Men and Women in North America. *Management Research Group Paper*

(4) Ibid

(5) Kram, K and McCollum (1995) "When Women Lead" Paper presented at ISPSO Symposium London *1995*

(6) Baker-Miller, J (1986) The New Psychology of Women *Beacon Press Boston, MA*

(7) Lieberman, S (1996) "When Men and Women Meet" Organisations and People *3;3 pp 20-24*

(8) Freud, S (1977) Some Psychical Consequences of the Anatomical Differences Between the Sexes. In Patrick C Lee and Robert Sussman Stuart (Eds) Sex Differences; Cultural and Developmental Dimensions *Urizen Books; New York*

(9) Tannen, D. (1996) Talking From 9 to 5 *Virago Press London*

(10) Gilligan, C (1982) In a Different Voice; Psychological Theory and Women's Development *Harvard University Press; Cambridge Mass*

(11) Frosh, S (1994) Sexual Differences: Masculinity and Ideology *Routledge; London*

Chapter 5

Helps and hindrances

- Enablers
- Blockers
- Balancing home and work life

In this chapter, we explore the external influences on these women's careers; the factors which have helped (i.e. 'enablers'), and the factors which have hindered (i.e. 'blockers'); and we consider how the women balance their home and work lives.

5 Helps and hindrances

Enablers

By enablers, we do not mean internal drivers, skills, qualities or attributes of these women, but those external forces which have facilitated the women's career progress either in the past or present.

Encouragement from family members and colleagues

"I could not do my job without my husband."

Director, Global Information Technology Company

Nearly all the women referred to the great support they received and continue to receive from family members, especially husbands and partners. Far from conforming to the stereotype of 'the single career woman with no one at home', 72% are married or partnered.

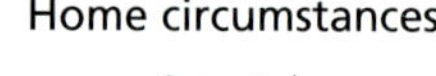

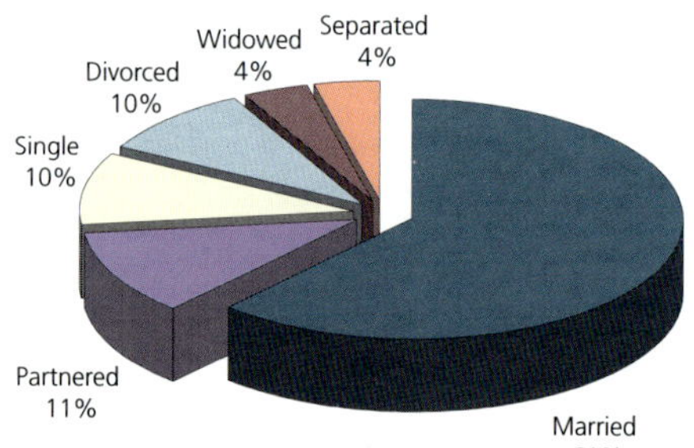

Figure 12

A number of the women said they had decided with their partners which of them should have the 'lead career' and, although most of their husbands/partners also worked, some were in less high-powered jobs. When it became clear whose career was progressing fastest, some husbands or partners chose to change their careers to less demanding roles, so as to be available to support their partners and/or take play a bigger role in caring for children. One woman said her husband had retrained as a teacher in order to be at home during the school holidays, when she could not take enough time away from work to be with the children herself. None of these women talked about 'having it all'. Many had made significant compromises to make their lives function more or less well, and many said they could not do what they did without the help of their husbands or partners.

This suggests a new twist on an old saying, viz. 'behind every successful woman, there is a successful man!' One woman said:

"The three most influential men in my life do not see a difference between what men and women do; my father, my brother and my husband. For my father's generation, this is particularly unusual. My husband is completely supportive and shocked by the bad behaviours of my colleagues and he appears to be totally relaxed about who earns the most money, who is travelling for business and so on."

Partner, Global Professional Services Firm

Others spoke of their debt to male and female work colleagues who opened doors for them:

"The Chair was very encouraging and supportive of women. He loved women! In this very male world, he was very supportive and said 'Give it time, it's an evolutionary process'. Other men didn't understand."

Deputy Chair, International Arts Organisation

"I have worked with wonderful men and really significant women. I am very aware of genders and the part they played in opening doors for me. The men have been supportive, gentle and ashamed of unfairness. The significant women have been powerful and concrete. I have an equal sense of gratitude to the men and the women."

Principal, College of Further Education

This last woman highlights men with 'feminine' and women with 'masculine' traits as being helpful to her in developing her own identity as an effective leader.

Guidance from role models, mentors and coaches

"The people I am close to at work are all women."

Director, Global Information Technology Company

Remarkably few of the women have had formal mentoring or coaching, and many of them commented on the lack of female role models to help create a vision of what they could become. Those women who have found support of that kind talk about how helpful it has been:

"There is no formal network of top women at my company. I bump into them and we can get close quickly. I have a female mentor, who is a successful businesswoman in the States. She ran her own consultancy firm."

Director, Global Information Technology Company

"I believe in being the ultimate at what I do, in doing the impossible. I have *two* coaches!"

Managing Director, Global Information Technology Company

"My division of the civil service took only one fast streamer per annum. I was only the second they had ever had. The division didn't choose me – I was allocated. I was a novelty as a woman and they couldn't have been nicer! It felt as though I had got lots and lots of uncles!"

Senior Civil Servant

'... LOTS AND LOTS OF UNCLES'

Lack of role models

But we have plenty of role models

"There is no female role model. I was only the third women ever, at my grade, to have maternity leave!"

Assistant Director, Civil Service

While the women were inspired by role models when they found them, many of them spoke of a lack of people to admire and identify with, male or female:

"In a masculine organisation, it's like learning to do everything with your left hand or in a second language. You learn to influence and cope with being in a bit of a foreign country. The few women who have prospered in the company have tended to be a bit eccentric – who do you learn from when all the role models are men who push their hands into their trouser pockets?"

Director, Transportation Company

Few natural networks

"Men have a club – drinking and playing golf. It is difficult to develop close friendships with men without a sexual connotation."

Director, Global Information Technology Company

Everyone else had trouser pockets

Women working in the more 'traditional' organisations, for example in transport, financial services and manufacturing, spoke of the difficulty of the lack of natural networks that they feel male colleagues create more easily, not least because at senior levels, males are in a large majority. Some of them spoke of their dislike and discomfort with networking in pubs or on golf courses and often felt excluded from the informal influencing systems in their organisations:

"One of the difficulties was not having a natural network, because it is a male dominated industry. Women can't ask men to pull them through as your male colleagues could. The lack of self-confidence has slowed me down at certain points. It can provide a barrier to getting the opportunities. If I had international business experience earlier on in my career, I would have gone further, faster. Staying in one organisation for such a long period of time has slowed my career."

Executive Manager, Global Telecommunications Company

Women in this research appear to have succeeded by refusing to recognise obstacles. Their determination appears to have been their biggest ally. Self-doubt linked with inhospitable organisational cultures seems to have prevented most of them asking for more support. Whatever the reasons, support was not made available. We noted that very few women spoke of any 'glass ceiling' on women's achievements at work, perhaps because they simply did not recognise one existed or had broken through it satisfactorily. They have clearly been helped greatly by whatever encouragement did come their way.

This normally came in a somewhat haphazard fashion, and some of the women have made up the shortfall by getting additional support from home. If more aspiring women had more formal support within their organisations to help them to create a future vision and 'buccaneer a bit' with their careers, it may be that their career progress would be faster, and maybe other women who otherwise would drop out of the race might be encouraged to stay. A reduction in women's leaving rates (especially at senior levels) would enable organisations to get a return on the investment they have made.

Balancing home and work life

The questions about the work/life balance yielded a mass of data. Everyone had something to say on this topic.

Work can dominate home life

“It's much more about work; 80% work and 20% personal is my time split.”

Board Director, FTSE 100 Company

For many of the women in our research, work can dominate home life and some seem to accept this, if somewhat reluctantly.

“I don't have a life outside of work. I travel about a week to 10 days per month. My social life is restricted to the weekends. I find it very hard to say 'no' to work responsibilities and that would take precedence over social things.”

Senior Scientist, International Pharmaceuticals Company

“I have consistently yearned after balance! I don't believe that for me this is possible. So long as I have this job, I am cheating at home in favour of work. People issues are often time sensitive; you must act when things are happening. So long as you are enjoying what you are doing, and you and your partner are comfortable with it, it doesn't matter which way it is split. I think it is important that it works for you both.”

Main Board Director, FTSE 100 Company

"It's a very finely balanced contraption."

Director, Global Information Technology Company

Some women talked movingly about their struggles to maintain balance in their lives, and the fact that their organisations can be unsupportive, especially if they have children:

"There aren't enough hours in the day! What happens; if all is well at home, there is no problem. The nature of work is that you feel a need to honour all those commitments. But if there are stresses at home, like the housekeeper is ill for a week or a child is sick, it throws the whole thing out. Both are a cathartic release for the other, so if everything is ghastly at work, it is lovely at home and vice versa. You hope you don't get the rotten things both times, both places. If you are a working mother, things work on a tight shoestring. If one thing goes out, it takes a lot of energy to cover the gap. Home tends to suffer. Work culture means you must be seen to be there. There was a huge suspicion at my company that people working from home weren't really working."

Functional Head, Transportation Company

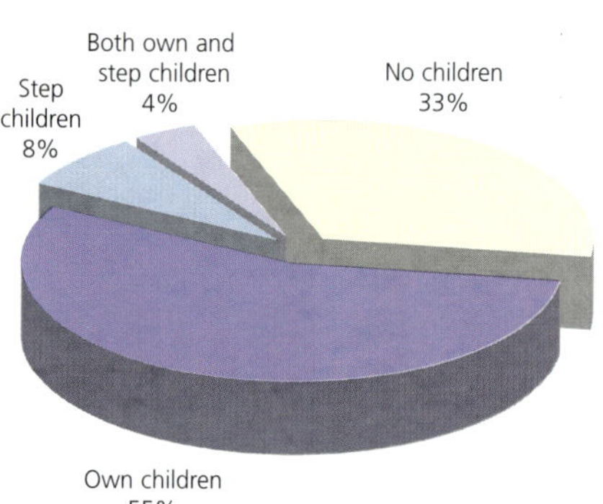

Figure 13

It may come as a surprise that, though heavily committed to their careers, 67% of our 52 women have responsibility for parenting their own and/or stepchildren (see Figure 13). The 52 women have a total of 59 children between them. They have tended to become mothers between the ages of 25 and 34, so these women have tended to have their children at about the same age as the general female population. (see Figure 14).

Many of these women are also involved in the labour intensive early years of being a parent, as can be seen from Figure 15 which shows their children's ages. Twenty seven of the women have their own children and, between them, they are responsible for 39 children under the age of 18, some whom are very young indeed.

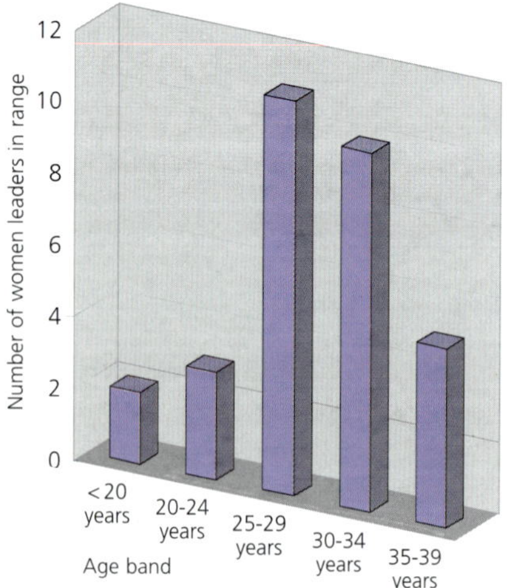

Figure 14

Many of the women place a high priority on their roles as parents, aim to keep a sensible balance, and achieve it at least some of the time, with a complex system of support, especially from husbands.

"Some would say having children is why women can't make it to the top. Women are not completely single-minded. I am involved with my children's lives and I will continue to do that even if the share price is dropping!"

Main Board Director, FTSE 100 Company

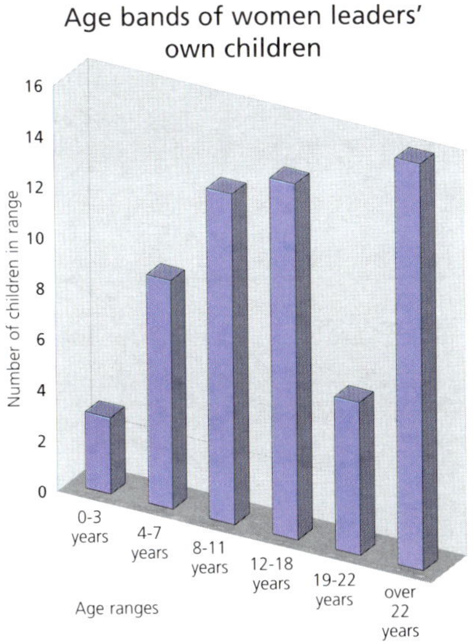

Age bands of women leaders' own children

Number of children in range: 16, 14, 12, 10, 8, 6, 4, 2, 0

Age ranges: 0-3 years, 4-7 years, 8-11 years, 12-18 years, 19-22 years, over 22 years

Figure 15

"I manage reasonably well, getting home when possible in time to see the girls and read them bedtime stories. Taking holidays is important, to have blocks of time. And I limit my evening engagements so I get home two evenings a week. I restrict my trips away and go for the shortest possible time. I do resent having to do chores. I find myself sorting out the washing at the weekend and thinking I bet my senior male colleagues don't have to do this!"

Director, Multinational Media Company

"I couldn't do my job without my husband. He looks after the children. He is there, he is the mum and my equivalent of the wife. He puts the kids to bed and goes to parents' evenings. I try very hard to do these things and have been quite successful but in the last year, the balance has skewed towards work and this is not good. My home life is very supportive to my company but not vice versa. My husband is comfortable because I try hard to be there. If he felt he was being taken for granted, he would be unhappy."

Director, Global Information Technology Company

None of these women feel it is possible to 'have it all', nor do they particularly strive for this. Their aspirations are typically more modest.

The beneficial effects of a stable home on work life

"Life at home is the source of strength and balance which enables me to be more courageous at work."

Senior Civil Servant

Women described the overwhelmingly positive impact of a strong and stable home life on work:

"I just love being married and I adore being a mother. It is just fantastic! My home life has been very beneficial to work. Being a mother, you learn a lot which is very important and you bring those skills into work life. I think being a mother gives you a different set of priorities which is very important to have in the work setting too."

Chief Executive, International Leisure Company

"Home influences work enormously beneficially. If you have daughters who put 'Do you know how awful it is to live with the 41st most influential woman in Britain?' on the fridge, it recharges common sense batteries!"

Chief Executive, National Not-for-Profit Organisation

But one woman commented:

"I don't think you can leave work out of home or home out of work. At home, I do talk about work, though nothing confidential. You do bring the tensions from work home. Sometimes I am so frustrated at work, I come home and almost kick the furniture! I find it hard to switch off and relax at home. And I don't have the stresses of bringing up a family that many of my female colleagues have. My work affects my home life much more than my home life affects my work. It is almost assumed that if you don't have children, you have more time for work. I think it is almost harder to relax so you need more free time to relax. Married friends don't agree with me! If you are single with no children, it is very easy for work to take over."

Board Member, International Professional Services Firm

Redesigning work lives

"A four day working week – that's my idea of heaven."

Chief Executive, Not-for-Profit Organisation

All the findings so far described are not, perhaps, surprising. Increasing numbers of men would say similar things if asked about work/life balance. However, we were interested to discover that the women had strong ideas on what to do to make achieving the balance easier. Many of them spoke about the fact that the traditional working week with two day weekends had been designed by men many years ago, for historical reasons that do not match up to the current needs of either men or women. They spoke of their longing for a shorter working week; that some of them do five days' work in four days, anyway, and only get paid for four! They said male colleagues often resisted their suggestions for working shorter hours actually at work on the basis that it would set a precedent and 'everyone would want to work like that'. These women feel everyone should be given the opportunity to do so. They did not feel a re-structuring of work lives to give people more time at home would lead to a lack of commitment to work but that a recognition of men and women in their wholeness as individual people would actually foster greater commitment in working hours.

Considering the factors which have helped and hindered women in their career alongside the ways in which they manage the home/work balance, two impressions emerge. If the women have been held back at all it has been due to a combination of self-doubt and lack of support from their organisations. What came first, the self-doubt or the lack of support? How might these two themes be related?

The women provided strong evidence that features of the organisational culture (Chapter 6) can have a powerful influence on what women are able to achieve. For instance, people's behaviour in organisations may deflate women's confidence:

"People in the workforce are waiting for you to collapse at work, almost taking bets on when that will be when you are juggling these bits of life. They are not there offering support to you. How can you do a presentation when you haven't slept through the night? You need the support to get through."

Managing Director, Executive Search Firm

The envy that people feel towards those in leadership positions may play a part here, though of course envy is not directed only at women. "Envy is an angry feeling that another person possesses and enjoys something desirable – the envious impulse being to take it away or to spoil it" *(1)*. Envy is directed towards men or women in leadership positions because they are seen to possess power, influence and perhaps wealth too. Those most idealised or most elevated are most likely to be deposed. Football managers and highly-paid, high profile Chief Executives alike spring to mind. Leaders' capacity to survive will partly depend on their ability to manage these strong negative projections and to mobilise strong positive ones for their own benefit.

Stokes *(2)* points out that envious attacks on male leaders will generally be around traits such as money-making, quality of decision-making, defining strategies, etc. all of which represent areas of masculine potency. Attacks on women centre on their feminine potency, on things like their appearance, creativity or reproductive and parenting ability. Media portrayals of women leaders with children as 'superwomen', or 'having it all' reinforce envy rather than create role-models – especially when women who lose out in Boardrooms are often portrayed by the same media as being forced to leave the Boardroom to get back to their 'neglected' children!

The attacks on men may be felt as more distant or external to them, focusing often on professional skills, competence, etc., while attacks on women are more personal, focusing on their mothering roles (for example); they may be experienced as more fundamentally destructive. The fear of such attacks from others may unconsciously discourage some women from taking up leadership roles or may lead them to 'bale out' as soon as they have children. It is important for organisations who do not wish to lose talented women to provide explicit support for women in leadership positions especially those who have children, whether this is in the form of flexible working hours, support for childcare or personal coaching.

References: Chapter 5

(1) Klein, M (1975) Envy and Gratitude *Hogarth Press; London*

(2) Stokes, J (1994) What is Unconscious in Organisations? *In R Casemore, G Dyos, A Eden, K Kellner, J McAuley and S Moss (Eds)* What Makes Consultancy Work:Understanding the Dynamics *South Bank University Press; London*

My baby's worth more than my £1/4m salary

Mother love – it's the real thing

Women still face uphill trek to place on board

Women fight for pension rights

Women put pressure on the glass ceiling

The number of female executives may be rising, but their progress to the boardroom is still slow, the survey shows

Why women make better managers

'I felt so mistreated by male colleagues that I just had to resign'

Dixons recruits 'superwoman'

Bye-bye baby, I'm off to work again

Women on course for top posts in management

Extending the shelf life of women

Chapter 6

The impact of organisational culture

- Being a "lone voice"
- Being "given courage, strength, knowledge and 'kick', money and opportunity to build a good career"
- What it is like at the top
- Transition: breaking the pattern of the past
- Culture change: the impact of women leaders

None of the women interviewed was self-employed. All worked in organisations; many in very large organisations. Organisational culture, therefore – that "soft, holistic concept with, however, presumed hard consequences" (1) – was very important to these women. Almost all of them regarded it as being a significant factor in their sense of effectiveness and well-being at work, and hence critically important in their success.

6 The impact of organisational culture

This chapter examines what the women leaders said about the culture of the organisations in which they work. It looks at what they said about the impact upon them of being few in number in the upper echelons of the organisation, about the benefits and the disadvantages of being one (or one of few) in what one of the women leaders said sometimes felt like "a foreign country". Staying with her metaphor, we then reflect on their descriptions of the characteristics of that foreign country: the terrain, the climate, the mores of the other inhabitants. Finally, the impact that these relatively new inhabitants of the upper strata are themselves having upon the cultures of the organisations in which they work is considered.

First of all, and looking back to Chapter 2, what are the organisations in which these women lead actually like? Twenty-five of the women leaders worked in large organisations. By "large" we mean organisations with above £500M turnover or, in the case of the public sector, with more than 1000 employees. Another nineteen women worked in medium-sized organisations of between £50M and £500M turnover or with between 100 and 1000 employees.

Forty-four of the women we interviewed were working at a level at which there were few other women in equivalent positions. The exceptions were those working in the NHS, where there are more senior women in top executive positions, and in the not-for-profit sector. For most there was a strong sense of professional life being a series of pioneering steps, in as much as they experienced themselves as one of a small number of women among many men.

We have seen in Chapter 2 the seniority of the roles that these 52 women leaders hold. 80% of them hold Main Board Directorships or Senior Civil Service positions. 63% of them hold the top position, by which is meant Chair, Chief Executive, Regulator, Managing Director, Permanent Secretary, senior member of Government. All the women we interviewed are the business equivalent of "household names" in their sectors.

Being a "lone voice"

These women are holding down very senior jobs in their organisations, and the majority, in large organisations. What is it like? Something that emerged very vividly from the interviews was the fact that they are, most frequently, the only woman at their level. This sense of being a lone female voice, or one of very few female voices, was a significant factor in the organisational cultures these women inhabit, and was something many of them commented upon.

"I got the Director's job out of 215 who applied. It was mould-breaking. The organisation had never had a female director before. It was a very exciting time."

Chair, Non-Departmental Public Body

"When I started going to Executive Team meetings there were 22 men. I was the only non-secretarial woman on the 4th floor. I did that for two and a half years."

Former Human Resources Director, Transportation Company

Some women described leadership teams in which there was greater balance.

"There are 3 men and 3 women in the top rank; 70% men and 30% women in the next rank."

Chief Executive, Local Authority

"There is a good balance of men and women. In my top team, there are two men and two women."

Managing Director, European Financial Services Firm

Being "given courage, strength, knowledge and 'kick', money and opportunity to build a good career"

Several women specifically mentioned the way in which they had been supported by others within the organisation as they took up their leadership roles. These people had exercised an influence upon the women's careers in ways subtly different from the "enabling" provided by family members or mentors (described in Chapter 5). Many women spoke warmly of a climate of encouragement within the organisation; and of the way in which they had been quite specifically "talent spotted", developed, and brought on in career terms by others who were often senior men:

“In the early days, I was lucky that I had people who were keen to support and promote women. My first boss was female, the first at her level. She was an extremely nice, lovely lady. In those days, it was still very much the [stereotype of the] strong, male leader who ruled with a rod of iron ...”

Managing Director, European Financial Services Firm

“[There have been] people who took an extraordinary level of interest and who gave me courage, strength, knowledge and ‘kick’; money and opportunity to build a good career.”

Chief Executive, International IT Staffing and Solutions Company

“Individual people who have been my bosses have given me the feedback that there is a next step and a next step. I have had to make those moves on my own, but the feedback was very influential: they have all been men.”

Chair, Non-Departmental Public Body

What it is like at the top

The encouragement and enthusiasm of senior people have clearly been important to many of these women, giving them that “courage, strength, knowledge and ‘kick’”. We noted too that many of the women leaders are now replicating with their own staff the beneficial patterns of behaviour they themselves experienced.

But they were also keenly aware that simply by being a woman in a leadership role, they were under a brighter-than-usual spotlight. Several women spoke of their feelings about finding themselves very visible and the centre of media attention. Most did not like it much, although one or two enjoyed it.

“I enjoy influencing and being close to power. Visibility, getting on with men in power, helping to articulate what we’re doing. Doing the things that scare you. Personal visibility. It’s about moving out of your comfort zone.”

Former Human Resources Director, Transportation Company

“I have been in interesting, changing organisations. I have been in a lot of acquisitions. I have had an international theme all through ... I think being a woman has been hugely positive. It does mean you are visible.”

Main Board Director, FTSE 100 Company

High visibility, media attention, almost always being the only woman in the room, are characteristics of the organisational “world” that these women leaders inhabit. Another characteristic of the organisational culture, for some of them, was opposition, or something similar. This was usually not explicit, given that they had been appointed by people who were presumably aware that they were women. It was implicit, and usually very subtle. Listening to many of our interviewees, we came to the conclusion that it was as if a number of organisations had appointed some of these women to the board or senior management group, but were then somehow disconcerted by the fact that they were not men and did not have male patterns of behaviour.

"Leaders do tend to choose people like themselves, so the senior men often choose other men to develop. One woman recently was told that she couldn't do a management job because she is a woman! They need to become aware that not everybody has to look like the person they see in the mirror first thing in the morning."

Executive Manager, Global Telecommunications Company

"I have been physically threatened at work. I was pushed up against a wall by a male Board Director, a peer. He poked me in the chest with his finger and said, "Who do you think you are?". I think this will not happen for the next generation of women. Perhaps this is because I have worked with a lot of men in their 60's, who did not have equal numbers of women with them at University, and so on. They weren't used to having to deal with women on an equal footing. This upcoming generation have much more equal numbers of men and women around them. In the future, it will be different for women coming though."

Chief Executive, International Leisure Company

"I was the first woman in the top team, before we became directors. In the beginning I had 10 managers reporting directly to me, all middle-aged men, and 200 staff. My predecessor had been a man of 55 with grey hair. I was a visible catalyst for change in the company and some people didn't like it. It felt like there was a lot of resistance to women in the company at the time."

Former Human Resources Director, Transportation Company

"In the main, I have worked for highly capital-intensive, very male dominated, very technical companies. I have always been one of very few women. There is an inbuilt sense of what a good manager looks like: another man, with all his good qualities. When the role models are all male, it is the biggest inhibitor of senior women being accepted in a company. It is harder to budge than if it were a deliberate prejudice."

Functional Head, Transport Company

“I believe that there is a fundamental difference in language and vocabulary between men and women. I have been in the boardroom, when I have said something and none of the men have reacted. Then a male colleague will translate from ‘womanspeak’ to ‘manspeak’. On the next day, a man will say the same thing, but in different words, and suddenly the male board members will respond to it, when they hadn't the day I said it. It has been very frustrating for me at times.”

Chief Executive, International Leisure Company

These quotes are a representative selection only. Organisational culture was something that figured very significantly in the descriptions the women leaders gave of their working lives; they spoke about it a lot. With very few exceptions, the women we interviewed identified culture, particularly at the top of the organisation, as being the hardest thing they had to deal with. This is a significant finding, and one which may underpin the work of other researchers, who have found that in the 1980s and 1990s many women have been actively questioning the values of the corporate world, and ‘voting with their feet’ by leaving large organisations in favour of self-employment *(2)*.

Transition: breaking the pattern of the past

Many of the women had a keen awareness of the power of history in the organisational cultures they inhabit. For some a significant structural change like the reshaping of whole industries as a result of privatisation, merger or acquisition had kick-started a process of large-scale change in the organisation in which they worked. Many women working in organisations that had been affected in this way had witnessed a cultural shift of major proportions, and a tension between an old and a new way of working. One main board company director in an industry subject to major restructuring described the associated cultural shift as being like watching an old world dying and a new one being born.

Similar reflections on the impact upon cultures of large-scale change were made by women executives in the public sector, where the structural changes of the 80s and 90s, such as the creation of Next Steps Executive Agencies, privatisation and the establishment of internal markets has had a similar effect *(3)*.

Organisational cultures are at once very fragile and extremely robust. Their fragility is associated with the balance between employees and their employing organisations. This delicate balance, both an outcome and a determinant of the relationship between the two, shapes the implicit and explicit linkage between the two groups. It constitutes a psychological contract *(4)* and is based on trust and consent *(5)*, *(6)*. But trust and consent have come under heavy fire in UK organisations in the last decade. Cultural changes occasioned by the structural changes described above have in many cases altered the balance of the psychological contract between social groups in organisations, sometimes in ways we are only just beginning to understand.

The causes of the shift in balance are easier to glimpse. The need to provide shareholder value rapidly after a merger or acquisition, or the restructuring that follows business process re-engineering, frequently drive cost reduction processes which result in 'downsizing'. 'Downsizing' has changed the psychological contract. Employers no longer guarantee job tenure and security, and in the absence of those historic givens, employees have learned to feel little loyalty to job or employer.

What the best employers offer as part of the new psychological contract is a new form of security, "employability", defined as the opportunity to learn, and in particular the provision of portable skills which better equip employees (now necessarily more mobile) to find work elsewhere. This represents a shift from a parent-child model founded on clear rules and expectations. It is a move away from the provision of "care" and security in return for labour and attachment ("You look after me and I'll be good and do this for you") to an adult-adult model. One which assumes that the "children" (or employees) will make provision for themselves to ensure their continued prosperity and employability, should their present employment cease *(7)*.

By no means all organisations have "renegotiated the contract" by offering employees the opportunity to learn, or by providing 'portable skills'. Of those that have, some have failed to make clear the linkage between that provision and the changed circumstances that have stimulated it. In not imposing the context they have not helped their people make sense of their changed reality. This is a failure of leadership *(8)*.

In any case, rational explanation of major cultural change does not of itself ensure that the changed circumstances are understood – or, even if understood, that they are accepted. Changing organisational culture is not only a *cognitive* process, it is visceral. Going back to Fukayama's concept of trust and consent, while people in an organisation may cognitively understand and support the rationale for the change, they may be very far from understanding and accepting it at the emotional level. Although rarely cited as a management thinker Pascal has nonetheless, we think, got it right: "the heart has its reasons of which the mind knows nothing ..." *(9)*.

What do this cultural fragility and the shift in psychological contract have to do with the cultures and climates within which these women are operating? They are important because they are linked with the second of the characteristics of organisational culture robustness, which is having significant impact upon the women leaders.

The robustness of organisational cultures lies in the tenacity with which old beliefs and behaviours endure. There is frequently a period, sometimes lengthy, during which strategic and structural changes (such as those described earlier) are pushing the organisation in one direction, and existing patterns of organisational behaviour are pushing it in another. In these circumstances it can take a very long time for a new set of beliefs and behaviours to have an impact upon the life of the organisation, and the disjunction between the new and the old can create its own kind of chaos. This is especially the case where major changes take place without a conscious effort by the organisation's leader(s) to create a new or modified culture.

All the men and women who lead in organisations are an integral part of this dynamic: major actors upon a changing stage. At any point in time, some will be part of the old world, some part of the new. Major structural changes and their outcomes do not discriminate. They are gender-neutral, they affect everyone. But as we observed earlier, many senior women are (often unwittingly) pioneers: **they are part of the new by virtue of the fact that they were not part of the old.** They inhabit organisational cultures which they had no hand in shaping. When those cultures undergo a seismic shift, senior women are not seen by others as being irrevocably aligned to the old way of doing things. They have less ego invested in the way things used to be. They are, and they see themselves as, part of the new.

But old ways of doing things are tenacious. They are familiar, the tools which come readily to hand. Organisational cultures have been shaped by people who have handled those tools with skill and dexterity. Many of the women leaders described organisational cultures that were in transition. They were still characterised by one particular set of values and norms, whilst at the same time espousing another set. This organisational schizophrenia can mean that, for example, an organisation can promote a woman to the Board and genuinely welcome that appointment, and at the same time manifest organisational behaviours that make it very hard for her to succeed. This can occur in a number of ways; some tangible, others less so.

The tangible ones were easier for the women leaders to define. The impact of working long-hours or "presentacism", and the difficulty of understanding inexplicit "rules" and (male) behavioural norms were mentioned by some women:

"Getting to be a partner was hard: knowing how to fulfil the criteria. I felt very isolated. And some unreasonable demands were placed upon me, such as at one point I didn't get a pay rise. I complained about this. I worked long hours, but I was told that I wasn't in the office until 10 or 11 pm when I had no work to do. I was expected to be here in case a client rang up and needed to have work done! Another, male, colleague – younger and more junior than me – did do that sort of thing, and I refused to do it. "

Partner, City Law Firm

Issues relating to behaviour were less tangible, and therefore more difficult to describe. The values of an organisational culture are shaped by those who control it, and in the past, women have not controlled organisations. The expectations of people in the organisation (and in particular, the expectations of senior people who have had more years in senior posts in which to formulate their expectations) about what "leadership" constitutes and what leaders look like, have been affected by what they have seen in the past. In the past, they have not seen women in leadership positions. They may as a consequence see what women do as managing rather than leading, purely because it is different from the way in which they have historically led as men.

An early study of advice given to women in an era when they were just starting to move into managerial roles in US corporates found that that they were being urged to be "more strategic, assertive and competitive and less emotional and sensitive". In addition women were supposed to wear three-piece, navy skirt suits, play golf, and "possess a thorough knowledge of professional sports." *(10)* At first reading this quotation seems archaic, but fifteen years later the question of what might be "appropriate" appearances and behaviour patterns for women leaders is still a moot point:

"Often the women who are most successful are those who manifest many of the same qualities as the senior men. There is one senior woman colleague, very undervalued, and quite brilliant, but no-one will make her a director. She is so able, but she doesn't fit the image of what a director should look like..."

Functional Head, Transport Company

"When I became Chairman I succeeded an exuberant and able Chairman. He was physically big, and he'd come into a room and dominate it, whereas I used to say "that's a very good piece of work, if I may say so". I was self-deprecatory, and now I am not. Circumstances forced me into a very high profile in the organisation, I changed. I became used to walking the talk, standing up and explaining why."

Senior Civil Servant

Some of the women described organisational cultures with which they were not comfortable; and in particular a competitive, macho style which they associated with swaggering or bullying:

"This culture values the table thumpers. The quick decision making. Action oriented. Forceful. It doesn't address the different leadership styles between the genders. It never came out that you can be a leader without being 'typically male'. The organisation sees female leadership styles as 'management' and male leadership attributes as 'leadership'. So influencing skills, thinking before you speak, understanding that people have different needs are seen as 'management' skills, not leadership."

Senior Scientist, International Pharmaceuticals Company

"It's a macho environment. It rewards ego, and empire-building, and selfishness. It's a strong sales culture. It hasn't the first idea how to reward someone who is not primarily motivated by money. I value being thanked and recognised. I think that is a gender thing?"

Director, Global Information Technology Company

A number of women described cultures characterised by sporting metaphors

"It is an open culture. Communicative. Personal. Friendly. Strong. Masculine. That is there still, despite a massive influx of women. There is still a masculine ethos in the company. Staff are still comfortable with a macho style: rugby and football metaphors in presentations, references to the sort of things that men tend to have in common. X's whole legacy was masculine – being very clear, very much in charge, being able to be matey in a blokish sort of way, exuding authority."

Former Human Resources Director, Transportation Company

"My own experience is that many men can't express emotions. Their anger and dissent doesn't get expressed, it's suppressed. And there's a kind of unreconstructed behaviour, particularly around sport. Men use sport as a means of being men together."

Former Director, Multinational Media Company

OF COURSE, THE M.D. WILL BE IMPRESSED BY MY OLD SCHOOL TIE... CRICKET... RUGGER BLUE ... ALL THAT OLD BOY NETWORK STUFF

The women leaders described ways of being which they did not share with male board-level colleagues:

“The organisation is a club. You are in or out. Women have ended up in the senior roles by accident. They don’t notice you are female if you are competent but they don’t want us to have a voice. Then they notice and don’t like it. It doesn’t feel male dominated except when decisions are taken. Then there’s a dual decision-making process: what happens in the Board, and the underground decisions made in the in-group that functions. There aren’t any women in the in-group. It’s a sales-focused, male dominated environment.”

Director, Global Information Technology Company

Many of the women described organisational structures and cultures based on military or social hierarchy with some of the patterns of behaviour associated with hierarchy, such as respect for seniority and positional power per se, and ‘command and control’:

“Until recently, the culture was ‘command and control’, pseudo-militaristic. Top-down and instruction based. It was very well managed in a tightly controlled way. We realised that there were a lot of changes happening – and more would be happening – and that it would be hard to deal with. We took a conscious decision to change.”

Senior Civil Servant

“The company is led by Anglo-Saxon males, even though it is an international company. They have been in the company all their lives. They don’t listen. They protect their turf. They are workaholics. Technically, they are the best. They are not very business oriented, and they are out of touch. And there’s a type of ‘institutional racism’. There is no diversity at top management level. Nationally and by gender.”

Senior Scientist, Global Oil and Gas Company

“This organisation is part feudal, part modern management theory-driven. It’s an uncomfortable mixture. It can be informal, friendly, and tolerate no pulling of rank, but the hierarchical aspects are deeply embedded. There are kings and barons, a world of distant, powerful folk. And a world order of scurrying folk, but we have tried to turn it sideways to introduce modern management practice.”

Executive Director, National Arts Organisation

They described organisations which were affected by politics and conflict:

"I admire X (Chief Executive). His board, including me, are good sales people but sometimes it feels like a viper's nest. And people see it. Very political and ego driven. X has the capacity to be a fantastic leader, but lets ego get in the way. People should want to die for him, but they don't."

Director, Global Information Technology Company

"The culture is very harsh. Not supportive at all. It's quite a macho organisation. There's no cohesive structure and the CEO got toppled. Conflict is never very far away and there's a great tendency to slip into adversarial positions. There is a macho style intolerance of failure. You need to be very tough. It's emotionally draining to engage and manage conflict."

Head of Function, Local Authority

The organisational cultures these women leaders described, albeit with some exceptions, did not seem to represent a fertile ground for innovation and creativity. A recent Coopers & Lybrand survey *(11)* identified preconditions for highly innovative organisations, such as ensuring that employees are encouraged to act as independent agents, and encouraging communicating through feelings, not just logic. Most of the women described cultures which were introspective, timid in their thinking, based upon out-dated concepts, unimaginative, over-focused upon numbers. They reflected upon the impact which cultures like these have upon creativity and innovation:

"The culture is enshrined by the phrase: 'we couldn't do that because it would set a precedent.' Even senior managers seem to believe that someone will smack their wrists if they make even a minor suggestion. There is a great resistance to try anything new. It is a lack of real empowerment."

Senior Scientist, International Pharmaceuticals Company

"The culture is people wanting spoon feeding, the world worked out for them. Not developing and learning. That's a dangerous way to run your life. I've had to give hard messages. ⅓ of the people will get on, ⅓ will mess about and ⅓ will leave. [The Company] must re-engineer itself into a professional services culture, but it isn't doing so. We want to be the Number One sales and services organisation by 2010 – but we can't do it without people. I don't believe we know how to achieve our ambition. There are lots of ways to do this. My way is one. People are key resources. Everything else is generic, hardware and software."

Director, Global Information Technology Company

"The culture is old-fashioned. Not risk-taking. Totally disconnected from the bottom line. It is strongly technically competent. It is inward-looking, unaware of external happenings and forces. It is a bit complacent and because of the drop in share price it's now scared. It's worried about the lack of leadership, and it's trying to change. But it is scared, and fear may block change and cause a reversion to old ways of doing things."

Senior Scientist, Global Oil and Gas Company

Balanced score-card approaches were perceived by many of the women to be introducing a more rounded way of evaluating performance and the success of an organisation. Some senior women executives are operating in top teams accustomed to focusing upon key financial ratios and not upon broader performance indicators. The approach is one they find frustrating and not ultimately successful:

"I was on the Board, but at Group level – the CEO – the real power was in his hands. We were treated appallingly badly, as puppets. Everyone was looking to me to do something. I was the filter between the horrendous top-level messages and the rest of the organisation. It was a huge company, but it lost all its good people including me. They made some stupid acquisitions ... the share price dropped from £9.5 to £1.65 in the space of seven months. Eventually the company was sold at £5/share. So everybody lost money. And its decline was entirely their fault; their inability to understand that it's people which make the difference. (The CEO) had the most appalling attitude towards people ... "

Chief Executive, International IT Staffing and Solutions Company

Culture change: the impact of women leaders

"THE PAST IS ANOTHER COUNTRY: THEY DO THINGS DIFFERENTLY THERE ..."

L.P. HARTLEY, THE GO-BETWEEN (PROLOGUE)

All the organisations in which the women leaders work are functioning in a climate of unremitting, fast-paced strategic change. This is likely to increase in the new millennium, which will itself stimulate different areas of change. The organisational consequences of global business development are just beginning to emerge as new issues to address.

As we noted in Chapter 1, things are different now, and will continue to be so. The future will be different and those responsible for leading organisations in both public and private sector will need new skills, qualities and attributes to continue to lead effectively. Large-scale structural changes like privatisation and deregulation have changed the whole context of work in the U.K.

Structural changes made here and in other developed economies have been emulated by economies elsewhere, which have in turn had an impact upon the western economies – a kind of 'bounceback' of cause-and-effect. *(12)*

The big waves of management action of the last decade such as mergers and acquisitions, cost reduction and downsizing have been driven by a need to respond to global competition and the threat to market share. They have been reactive. The need now is to take the initiative to create a climate nationally in which creativity and innovation can thrive. This agenda for change is examined more fully in the following Chapter. Here, we consider how women leaders are introducing cultural change to the organisations in which they work, seeking to play their part in moving things forward:

"It is an informal organisation. It doesn't stand on ceremony. X has always allowed each part of the organisation to have and enjoy its own culture. From an external perspective, we are judged as tough but respected. The organisation values drive, delivery, openness, energy, good communication skills, quite up-front leadership. This is quite an action-oriented company and you need to do your reflection in your own time. Innovation and creativity are important in our businesses."

Main Board Director, FTSE 100 Company

"The culture is success-oriented. A 'can-do' approach is encouraged and personal contribution is paramount. The organisation has a great ability to reinvent itself in line with market trends. The importance it attaches to the role of the individual is extreme, which is only beneficial if it is harnessed. So that the organisation has to have leaders who reinforce the framework that relates individual effort to the focus on the customer, first, and the need to be competitive, second."

Executive Manager, Global Telecommunications Company

"I was Deputy Chairman when we started down the culture change road, and I was influential in that. In the early days we identified two Departments and gave them freedom, within certain parameters, to do what they wanted. We as a Board backed them. There was no punishment. People gradually started to believe it. We have been 'teaching the elephant to dance'. Learning to be a leader was quite a journey, really."

Senior Civil Servant

There seemed to be something significant about the way these women are leading and the impact they are having upon organisational culture change. A large number of the women believed themselves to be pivotal in the process of change. For some that was a deliberate, conscious process as they sought actively to change systems, processes and ways of working in their organisations. For others, it was a by-product of their presence and therefore inadvertent. Simply by being there and getting on with their work, women in this latter group ensured that things were not the same as they were before.

"The culture is very values-driven. We concentrate on treating people as individuals, both staff and clients. We're always trying to do things better. I've had a "good ideas hot line" telephone installed on my desk, to try and promote good ideas and give people direct access to me. It's often used at weekends, I've found, when people have a chance to reflect. I have a call-minder on it. The ideas are of excellent calibre. Most people identify themselves and I always go back to them and thank them. I want to promote a real culture of flexibility and thanking."

Chief Executive, National Not-for-Profit Organisation

"We are in the midst of a big transition. The board is leading a great deal of change. It has been pretty practical, energetic, very tasky, very high standards, detailed, quite hierarchical. It is going to be very practical, open, flatter, more strategic at senior levels, customer focused, and still have high standards."

Main Board Director, FTSE 100 Company

"Leadership must now be all the way through the organisation, and if we are to be customer focused, everyone MUST be a leader. We need to set a framework but not give people the answers all the time. People need to have the opportunity to come up with their own answers. The culture must value diversity. We must be more tolerant about different ways of doing things, as long as the output is to the required standard."

Main Board Director, FTSE 100 Company

OH NO, WE DON'T HAVE ANYTHING LIKE **THAT** AT OUR COMPANY ...

"Traditionally, it's been an operational exercise, not strategic. Firefighting expertise and engineering skills were lauded. That is changing, but the process is quite slow. That is where a lot of women will have a significant role to play. The core business is contract management with a view to end-use customer. This is the measure by which everyone is accountable. Speed of response, the ability to handle many things at once, teamworking, facilitation (not command) and a genuine desire to please the customer are key. We are moving to a service culture, which is traumatic for some people."

Functional Head, Transport Company

"Through cultural transformation work we are doing, we are trying to get the whole organisation to learn to build relationships, to listen, to communicate more, rather than being task and functionally focused. Regardless of who you are, everybody is being encouraged to work in that way."

Managing Director, International Retailer

"Our industry is changing and growing fast. Our competitors are changing every day. Technology and the markets are changing. We are globalising. Unless we can let go and let people make their own judgements, we will lose out. None of us at Board level has enough wisdom to identify trends and to take action quickly enough for today's world. The corporate culture and leadership has to be enabling. You have to have a clear strategy and support framework to enable people to get there, for them to put flesh around the bones of the strategic frame you've set out."

Board Director, FTSE 100 Company

Sometimes intentionally, as part of corporate strategy, sometimes inadvertently, simply by being there and by leading in the way which seemed most natural to them, many of the women we interviewed were leading change in their organisations. We found considerable synergy between the leadership style the women leaders described themselves as using, and the leadership methods that leading management thinkers believe will be necessary for the successful organisations of the future.

We noted in Chapter 3 that one of the distinctive aspects of the women leaders interviewed was that they deployed their personal qualities and attributes as skills. What we mean by this is that who they are as people is a fundamental part of how they behave as leaders. Cooper and Sawaf describe this approach as "putting integrity to work" *(13)*. It is where women leaders find themselves operating in environments where they are unable, or where it is difficult, to put their own way of being, their own integrity, to work that they experience an inhospitable organisational culture.

The women we interviewed expressed themselves without exception as being uninterested in hierarchy, status (except insofar as it offered a platform for doing something), politics, pretence or intrigue. They were very interested in caring for people, establishing meaning and building the organisation around that; in networking, listening, enabling and allowing people to make their own judgements.

As we have noted some of the women leaders operating in organisational cultures that were inhospitable to these ways of working, and in those cases

References: Chapter 6

(1) Hofstede, G (1991) Cultures and Organisations: Software of the Mind *McGraw-Hill, Maidenhead, Berks (p.18)*

(2) See for example, National Management Remuneration Survey *(1994) Institute of Management London*

the women were "bumping into" the culture and sometimes getting bruised in the process. Many of the women were in a senior enough position to do something about it, and were doing so, like setting culture change work in place, modelling new behaviours, coaching their senior teams and challenging customs and practices inappropriate to a twenty-first century workplace.

Some women who were working in particularly unreconstructed organisational cultures felt abraded by the process and were thinking about leaving, not because they had ceased to be interested in the work but because of the unremitting stand-off between the culture and their values-base style of leadership. This was particularly noticeable in cases where women were using their style of leadership, within a holding company or larger entity. These women had succeeded in creating one type of organisation, often spectacularly successful against all formal performance indicators, which had to function within a larger "parent" group being run under quite different rules.

Reflecting upon what he had learned from four decades of teaching and research, one leading management thinker recently wrote

"We've gone about 50% of the way in terms of intellectual acceptance of participative management and employee involvement. Where we still need to go further is in the capacity of tough leadership to create a social architecture that will generate intellectual capital – ideas, innovations, learning, know-how. That's what it's all about." *(14).*

If he is right and that is 'what it's all about', then it is interesting that these women leaders are engaged in exercising tough leadership to create just such a social architecture. They are part of the new and like all harbingers of the new experience some of the negative as well as the positive implications of that role.

"You inevitably draw down a degree of hostility when you try to initiate change. You have to have a pretty strong sense of yourself not to be vulnerable."

Chair, Non-Departmental Public Body

The next chapter summarises issues raised by the findings of the research, and outlines a framework for action.

(3) Thomson, P (1995) "Aftermath: Making Public Sector Change Work – Part 1." Public Policy Review *Vol. 3, Issue 1*

(4) Kets de Vries, M F R "Leaders who make a difference" INSEAD Working Paper (95/24/ENT)

(5) Kouzes, James M and Barry Z Posner 1995) The Leadership Challenge, *Jossey-Bass San Francisco*

(6) Fukayama, F (1995) Trust: the Social Virtues and the Creation of Prosperity *Hamish Hamilton Ltd(6)*

(7) This idea is being challenged. Data collected in a longitudinal study (1990-1992) of the behaviour of six companies in an industry facing declining revenues and profits, during periods of cost reduction and strategic change suggest that during cost reduction and downsizing there is a substantial overall deterioration in the quality of management practices, with a particularly large drop in the dimension of responsibility (which involves both trust and the delegation of authority). See George Litwin, John Bray and Kathleen Lusk Brooke, Mobilising the Organisation, *(1996) Prentice Hall, Englewood Cliffs, N.J. (pp 229-231)*

(8) Taffinder, Paul (1995) The New Leaders: Achieving Corporate Transformation through Dynamic Leadership *Kogan Page, London*

(9) Pascal, Blaise (1576) Pensées *Garnier-Flammarion, Paris 1976*

(10) Loden, Marylin (1985) Feminine Leadership *Random House, New York*

(11) Coopers & Lybrand & Henley Management Centre (1997) Innovation Survey

(12) Tait, Ruth (1995) Roads to The Top *Macmillan Pres Ltd, Basingstoke, Hamps*

(13) Cooper & Sawaf (1997) Executive EQ: Emotional Intelligence in Business *London: Orion Business (pp 186-187)*

(14) Bennis, Warren (1998). Managing People is Like Herding Cats: Warren Bennis on Leadership *London, Kogan Page (p107). Warren Bennis in a recent book identifies the ability to demonstrate human values of empathy, trust, mutual respect – and courage – as critical determinants of leadership.*

Chapter 7

Issues raised by the research and practical actions to take

In our experience, work which throws a new light (or sometimes just a brighter light) on issues which have implications for organisational change sometimes attracts criticism because it offers no insight about *what practical things can be done* to implement such change. Mindful of this, we have included material which brings together from the preceding chapters the core issues raised and outlines the actions which could be taken to address them. It is structured around actions which could be taken by organisations and individuals in any sector. Before turning to this, we summarise below the issues raised by the research.

7 ISSUED RAISED BY THE RESEARCH AND PRACTICAL ACTIONS TO TAKE

Issues raised by the research

The failure to get women into senior management, and the failure to get women into the Boardroom were identified in 1990 as significant barriers to women's optimum participation in the UK workforce. Almost ten years later and on the threshold of a new millennium, women are becoming better represented in management. They are still significantly under-represented at Board level. In the words of that 1990 Report "if Boardrooms are where power and influence reside, then women are clearly excluded".

This matters. It matters on grounds of social justice and on economic grounds. The argument from social justice is, we imagine, self-evident nowadays. Just in case it is not, we affirm that any society which, through deliberate intent or through inertia, fails to offer all its citizens the opportunity to participate fully at every level of the national life in both public and private sector, is unjust. The economic argument is less principled. It states simply that an economy which through deliberate intent or through inertia fails to recognise and deploy effectively all its human capital is sub-optimal, and likely to be less competitive in world markets.

There are downstream reasons why having so few women exercising power and influence at the top of organisations is important. It matters because women's exclusion or presence in minimal numbers at very top levels results in organisations being lop-sided. The strategies being formulated for what happens in British life, in public and private sector organisations, in local and central government, are not being shaped by both men and women. The thinking and decision-making processes are not benefiting from all the brain power, insights, discrimination and judgement that is available.

One result of this lop-sidedness (the fact that the thinking and decision-making processes are not shared by both men and women) is that organisational strategies (what organisations do) and organisational cultures (how organisations are) are being shaped largely by men. This research suggests that the organisational cultures which have been and are being created may actually be inhospitable to women, which in turn may mean that women do not thrive and may choose to leave. So the situation may well be self-perpetuating: few women "coming through" to choose from; senior executive women taking a look at the inhospitable cultures at the very top of organisations and declining to get involved; few women therefore visible as role models to younger women ... and so on. This is, we affirm, an unsatisfactory cycle which needs to be broken. The few, but extremely able women whom we have interviewed need to be joined by many more. It needs to be completely normal to be a woman at the top.

Practical actions to take

There are six points, a mixture of direct action and philosophical stance, which are generic to all organisations, whether in public or private sector. They address the key finding revealed by the research, that against expectation and projections, ten years of gradual change have not significantly increased the number of women at the top and that further action is needed. These points are relevant to the Chairman, the Chief Executive, the Board or the public sector equivalent (those who set the tone of the organisation); and in the case of publicity-quoted companies should be of more than passing interest to shareholders. The points are:

1. Get more women into the top levels in organisations. Give no quarter. In the words of a current advertising slogan, "just do it". Look as a matter of urgency at the criteria being used for selection for those top jobs. Adjust them. Take a few calculated risks. Be bold in your appointments.

2. Get significant numbers of women into the top levels in organisations. Determine to break the pattern of the "lone voice" woman among a sea of men. Set some numerical goals and some time-scales.

3. Do not expect women to be like men in the way they:

- talk
- prioritise their activities
- arrive at decisions
- interact with people
- come to judgements.

This research found that women deploy their personal values, qualities and attributes as skills in their own right. Let women bring all of themselves to work.

4. Do not expect women to be perfect. Men are not, and there are some men at Board level who have been spectacularly unsuccessful in the way they operate. Some women will also be spectacularly unsuccessful. Perfection is not an option.

were philosophical about this. Others clearly found balancing home and work life more difficult. Structural change in the labour market, coupled with the lightning advance of IT, is forcing change in working patterns, so this may be a problem in the process of resolution. Establishing a work group or target team to focus on the redesign of work lives in your particular professional environment would speed the process, to advantage.

Arising from Chapter 6: (The impact of organisational culture)

(a) In the public sector the implications of the Nolan Report are being influential in opening up avenues of advancement for women. Examine the thinking behind Nolan and establish within the organisation a similar framework, communicating widely its purpose and intent.

(b) Build into the organisational competency framework the specific ability to "talent spot" able women. Appraise managers against this competence alongside their other competencies. Ensure managers know what they are looking for, in terms of women's leadership potential.

(c) Ensure that bright young people chosen to work in the 'cabinet office' of the executive team include young women as well as young men.

(d) Offer work shadowing of senior women to women in middle management.

(e) Give media training to senior executive women. During the period when women in top jobs are still the subject of intense media interest it is important that they be schooled in how to respond confidently to press and television enquiry.

(f) Women deploy their personal qualities, values and attributes as professional skills. How they are affects how they operate. Let them 'bring themselves to work' and work in ways which accept them as women.

(g) The women we interviewed identified culture, particularly at the top of the organisation, as being the hardest thing they had to deal with. Possibly the single most important step that organisations can take in addressing this issue is to recognise the extent of the problem. It is unlikely to be sufficient to make small isolated changes to HR practice or management practice, etc. Organisations will need the courage to face up to changing the paradigm: that is, to take a fundamental look at the way they do business and to make real changes.

Appendix I: Method

Research method

This work is based on qualitative research methods. It has involved exploring the experience of women in leadership roles, rather than in making attempts to measure that experience by capturing it in numbers. We are keenly alert to the dangers inherent in the approach we have chosen, especially with regard to the stance that the researcher adopts in questioning, interpretation, and to the whole process of enquiry. We have adopted procedures that are designed to minimise, or at the very least hold up to public view, anything that might skew the results in, say, the direction that our preconceptions dictated.

The term 'grounded theory' comes nearest to defining our approach (1); (2). It is about ways of handling, organising and analysing unstructured qualitative material. It is an approach which acknowledges the contribution of the researchers as participants in that process and their essential involvement in it. It means that a particular body of knowledge is grounded in or emerges from the experience of those involved in it, both researchers and participants, rather than being imposed from outside. If we are trying to understand people's experience, we do it by engaging with them in an exploration of what that experience is like for them – how they themselves see the world through their own eyes. At the same time, however, we have to be careful not to get sucked too far into the other person's world. Therefore we need to be able to maintain distance or separateness if the exploration is to be meaningful. We are seeking to make explicit what is otherwise taken for granted and, in doing this, generate new ideas. Features of qualitative data are:

- Consistency of outcome may be a feature, but the context may also form a very important part of the story – in this study, the fact that the subjects were exclusively women, and not men, was important; the women's organisational settings were sometimes crucial to the stories they told; and so on
- Making sense to the reader is important – the ideas should hang together in some way that evokes a response, even if this is disagreement
- Ideas on cause and effect may emerge but loose ends can be left
- Measurement is not necessary to the telling of the story
- The aim is interpretation, the possibility of going beyond the data

Problems of this method

1. The story is always going to be linked to its context. For example, the subjects are senior women, not junior women or men, this provides a challenge to going beyond the given.

2. Accounts and interpretations can never be conclusive. More may happen, so we can only capture a moment in time – a 'snapshot'.

3. The researchers' existing knowledge on the subject and the impact of the subject of study on the researchers generates a potential for distortion of the data.

Some solutions

Here are the steps we took to ensure the trustworthiness of the research – we:

- Adopted a clear approach everything we did was meticulously documented
- Took great care to produce a dependable structure for the actual face-to-face enquiry (see Appendix II) which did not strait-jacket the exploration
- Selected the participants to achieve a spread of experience – representing a diverse range of organisation sectors, sizes. This offers the potential for wide applicability of our findings
- Had a carefully designed project and identified individual responsibilities
- Used an interpretation process consisting of:

– producing an account from each individual meeting

– identifying the broad themes, individually for all accounts

– examining the account again for 'events' that cluster under the themes, in order to help refine them, to identify different levels of theme, and also to help illustrate them

– applying a similar content-analysis-based approach to the aggregate of themes across all interviewees, in order to identify both what is common to and distinctive about their experience

- Coupled with all this the application of quantitative measures where these were appropriate. For the most part, this applied to demographic data
- Found, by the writing stage, that it was possible to make links between the findings and other relevant work in the field

We learned a great deal about women in leadership roles from our participants, from the research process and from the ways in which we worked effectively with the data.

References: Appendix I

(1) Richardson, J (1996) Handbook of Qualitative Research Methods for Psychology and the Social Sciences *BPS Books, Leicester.*

(2) Hayes, N (Ed) (1997) Doing Qualitative Analysis in Psychology *Psychology Press, Hove, East Sussex.*

Appendix II: Interview Schedule

Basic Information

1 Name
2 Age
3 Role/position
4 Brief role/position description
5 Industry/enterprise/field of work
6 Length of time in present role

Family Background and Education

7 Father
(a) Name
(b) Occupation
8 Mother
(a) Name
(b) Occupation
9 Brother(s)
(a) Name(s)
(b) Occupation(s)
10 Sister(s)
(a) Name(s)
(b) Occupation(s)
11 Marital status:
Married Partnered Single
Separated Divorced
12 Husband/partner
(a) Name
(b) Age
(c) Occupation
13 Son(s)
(a) Name
(b) Age
(c) Occupation
14 Daughter(s)
(a) Name
(b) Age
(c) Occupation
15 School (main)
(a) Name
(b) Type
(c) Exam results
16 University(ies) – where applicable
(a) Name(s)
(b) Subject(s)
(c) Results

About Your Career

17 Career progress – occupation(s), employer(s), positions, with dates
18 What thinking, decisions, aims, have informed or influenced this progress?
19 What other factors have affected it, if any?
20 What plans or ambitions for its future do you have?

About Your Present Organisation

21 How would you characterise its culture, 'the way things are done round here'? What, if anything, is particularly significant about this – beneficial or otherwise?
22 What are relationships like in general – between bosses and subordinates, members of the organisation and their clients, men and women, and so on?
23 What kinds of leadership quality does it value?
24 How many men are there in leadership roles?
How many women?
25 How does it help people to attain leadership roles – or doesn't it?
26 Does it differentiate in this as between men and women?
If so, how?
And if not, should it?
27 What kind of leadership will it need in the future? And why?

About You

28 What, if anything, has had a particular effect in helping you to make progress in your career?
29 What, if anything, has got in the way of career progress?
30 To what extent do life at home and life at work each affect the other – beneficially or otherwise?
And what does the idea of a balance between these two mean to you?
31 What do you think you are particularly good at – at work or in life more generally?
32 And at what are you not so good?
33 How do others see you in these terms?
34 What particular sources of satisfaction do you have – in or outside your work?
35 And the dissatisfactions or frustrations?
36 To what extent do you think there is a gender effect in these?
37 What would you do to raise the satisfactions and reduce the frustrations?

About this Process

38 Is there anything we have missed, and if so what?
39 Is there anything we have covered that you don't think was appropriate for any reason?
40 How have you found it?

About the authors' companies

The Change Partnership Ltd. was founded in 1994 to provide customised development programmes for senior people. The focus has been to allow successful senior people the opportunity to work in real time on their business and life agenda with a personal coach of significant experience.

The Change Partnership is now a team of fifteen consultant directors based in London, Swindon, Warrington and Edinburgh.

Internationally The Change Partnership has offices in Brussels and Johannesburg and through The Global Coaching Partnership, expert coaching can be facilitated in North America, Denmark, Germany, Australia, New Zealand, Hong Kong, Shanghai and Singapore.

Personal development delivered in a one to one environment has proved highly beneficial to successful executives and directors and those with high potential.

The Change Partnership has also developed the facilitation skills needed for top teams, using coaching tools and techniques in a collective form.

THE TAVISTOCK CONSULTANCY SERVICE
Working below the surface

The Tavistock Consultancy Service is a unit within the world famous Tavistock Centre. Its team of psychologists specialise in consulting to the leadership of organisations across all sectors of the economy. It is unique in being part of a National Health Service Trust.

The distinctive competence of the Tavistock Consultancy Service is in working with psychological processes going on below the surface in individuals, groups and teams and in the whole organisation in order to:

- release intelligence about the emotional life of the organisation
- develop creative solutions to organisational dilemmas
- manage internal tensions
- enhance strategic leadership

The Tavistock Consultancy Service offers:

- One to one coaching with senior executives and their leadership teams
- A Development Portfolio of programmes such as 'Leading and Working with Teams', 'Developing Consultative Skills' and 'Strategic Leadership'
- Research into organisational dynamics.

ABOUT THE AUTHORS

Elizabeth Coffey is a Director of The Change Partnership Ltd where she works as a Senior Executive Coach.

Born in the USA of an Irish-American father, who was a Professor of Philosophy, and a Belgian Philologist mother, Elizabeth has always felt a strong affinity with Europe and traditions of developing people. These strands were further reinforced through twelve years of Steiner primary and secondary education. During five months travelling in Europe in 1984, she decided she felt so much at home that she would stay – and since that time has spent only six months in the USA.

After pursuing a "double major" in Psychology and English Literature at Wellesley College, and graduating cum laude, Elizabeth spent a few years in Harvard Medical School teaching hospitals in Boston, honing her research and counselling skills. She then shuttled for a while between London and Frankfurt where she settled. Since by then she had a small son, but could locate no suitable nursery school in Frankfurt, her immediate reaction was to found one. In typical fashion, once the school was well-established she teamed up with a friend and established a consultancy – Nexus GmbH – to design and deliver 'cross cultural' programmes to German companies such as BMW, to help their managers develop more effective global management skills.

Elizabeth moved back to London in 1995, and building on her earlier research and consulting experience, joined Saxton Bampfylde International plc to carry out director level executive searches across many business sectors in the UK and world-wide. In this role, she spoke with over 100 directors a month and in doing so built up an unusual depth of personal knowledge of the issues surrounding executives at the highest levels in industry, commerce and public services. This led to Elizabeth joining The Change Partnership Ltd in 1997.

Elizabeth dedicates her efforts in this work to her son, Alexander, with the wish that the seeds sown here will grow and ripen for his generation.

Clare Huffington is the Director of The Tavistock Consultancy Service. She is a Chartered Psychologist and trained family psychotherapist with over twenty years' experience in the field.

In her career, Clare has been a teacher, educational psychologist, university lecturer and clinical psychologist. Now she is an organisational consultant and senior executive coach.

Her approach to coaching clients is to create a safe and supportive setting in which they can challenge themselves and revive their personal creativity and capacity for innovation at work.

Clare's recent achievements include designing, setting up and co-ordinating a Europe-wide development programme for executives in a global IT company; working with lead partners in a 'Big 5' management consultancy firm to enhance board-level client work and collaborating in a needs analysis of senior executive development in an investment bank.

Clare has written seven books and a variety of articles on organisations, consultancy and the management of change.

Peninah Thomson is a Director of The Change Partnership Ltd where she works as a Senior Executive Coach.

Based in Paris, Peninah worked as an international civil servant to the Board of National Delegates of NATO in Rome, Paris, Washington and The Hague: a role which gave her unparalleled grounding in networking, negotiating, diplomacy, international relations, multi-cultural politics – and people.

She then went to Oxford to work on her DPhil, but after a few years which were a blend of research, academic administration and teaching, a Coopers & Lybrand report (A Challenge to Complacency) prompted her towards management consultancy.

The next eleven years with PricewaterhouseCoopers involved working with individual Chief Executives and Board members and with Boards as groups on strategy, organisational culture, and – critically – on leadership. Peninah also designed and delivered leadership development programmes for several FTSE 100 organisations, and was an adviser to the PwC Leadership Team on strategic leadership. Her public sector work included working at Cabinet level in the Governments of Kuwait, Singapore, India and Hong Kong and a spell on secondment to the UK Cabinet Office.

Peninah was educated at the Universities of Oxford, Grenoble and the Sorbonne, trained as a Counsellor at the American Hospital in Paris, and has worked on assignments in eleven countries. She is the co-author or author of several articles and three books on aspects of organisational change.

Bibliography

Acker, J (1987) Women and work in the social sciences. In A.H. Stromberg and S Harkness (eds) *Women working: theories and facts in perspective* Mayfield Publishing Co, Palo Alto, Calif.

Armstrong, M ed (1992) *Strategies for Human Resource Management: A Total Business Approach*. Kogan Page, London

Baker-Miller, J (1986) *The New Psychology of Women* Beacon Press, Boston, MA

Bennis, W *Managing People is Like Herding Cats: Warren Bennis on Leadership* Kogan Page, London

Bion, W (1967) *Second Thoughts: Selected Papers on Psychoanalysis* Heinemann, London

Blum, D (1998) *Sex on the Brain* Penguin, New York

Bryce, L (1989) *The Influential Woman* Piatkus, London

Cartwright, S & C Cooper (1992) *Mergers & Acquisitions: The Human Factor* Butterworth–Heinemann Ltd, Oxford

Catalyst (1998) *Advancing Women in Business* Jossey-Bass, San Francisco

Catalyst *1998 Census of Corporate Officers and Top Earners* (1998) Catalyst, New York

Catalyst *Census of Women Board Directors of the Fortune 500* (1998) Catalyst, New York

Catalyst (1996): Women in Corporate Business: Progress and Prospects Catalyst, New York

Chee, A (1999) "City Limits" *Securities and Investment Review* July/August

Collins, C (1994) *The Vision of the Fool* (ed. Brian Keeble) Golgonooza Press, Ipswich

Cooper & Sawaf (1997) *Executive EQ: Emotional Intelligence in Business,* Orion Business, London

Coopers & Lybrand & Henley Management Centre (1997) *Innovation Survey*

Covey, S (1992) *Principle-Centered Leadership* Simon and Schuster, London

Davidson, M.J. and Cooper, C.L. (1987) Female managers in Britain – a comparative perspective. *Human Resource Management,* Summer, 26

Equal Opportunities in the Civil Service: Data Summary (1998)

Feldman, M and M Spratt (1999) *Five Frogs on a Log: a CEO's Field Guide to Accelerating the Transition in Mergers, Acquisitions and Gut Wrenching Change* Harper Business, New York

Franks, S (1999) *Having None of It: Women, Men and the Future of Work*, Granta Publications, London

Freud, S (1977) Some psychical consequences of the anatomical differences between the sexes. In Patrick C Lee and Robert Sussman Stuart (Eds) *Sex Differences; Cultural and Developmental Dimensions* Urizen Books, New York

Frosh, S (1994) *Sexual Differences: Masculinity and Ideology* Routledge London

Fukayama, F (1995) *Trust: the social virtues and the creation of prosperity* Hamish Hamilton Ltd, London

Future Unit, DTI August 1999 – *Work in the Knowledge-Driven Economy* DTI, London

Gilligan, C (1982) *In a Different Voice: Psychological Theory and Women's Development* Harvard University Press; Cambridge, Mass

Goleman, D (1998) *Working with Emotional Intelligence* Bantam Books, New York

Halton, W (1999) Personal communication

Hamilton, K (1999) "The women who move Britain" *Management Today*, March

Handy, C (1997) *The Hungry Spirit* Random House, London

Hansard Society *Report of The Hansard Society Commission on Women at the Top* (1990), London

Hayes, N (Ed) (1997) *Doing Qualitative Analysis in Psychology* Psychology Press, Hove, East Sussex

Helgesen, S: *The Web of Inclusion* (1995) Doubleday, New York

Hirschhorn, L (1997) *Re-Working Authority: Leading and Following in the Post-Modern Organisation* MIT Press Cambridge, Mass

Hofstede, G (1991) *Cultures and organisations: Software of the Mind* McGraw-Hill, Maidenhead, Berks

Holton, V and J Rabbetts (1997) *Women on the Boards of Britain's Top 200 Companies 1997* Opportunity 2000

Institute of Management (1994) *National Management Remuneration Survey,* London

Kabacoff, R and Peters, H (1999) *Leadership and gender: a comparison of leadership style* Management Research Group Paper

Kets de Vries, M F R (95/24/ENT) "Leaders who make a difference" INSEAD Working Paper

Klein, M (1975) *Envy and Gratitude* Hogarth Press, London

Kotter, J P (1996) *Leading Change.* Harvard Business School Press, Boston, MA

Kouzes, J M and B Z Posner (1995) *The Leadership Challenge* Jossey-Bass, San Francisco

Kram, K and McCollum (1995) "When Women Lead" Paper presented at ISPSO Symposium London

Labour Force Survey, (Spring 1995, 1997 and 1999). Office for National Statistics, London

Lacan, J (1977) – *Ecrits: A Selection* Tavistock, London

Lieberman, S (1996) "When Men and Women Meet" *Organisations and People* 3:3

Litwin, G, J Bray and K Lusk Brooke, *Mobilising the Organisation* (1996) Prentice Hall, Englewood Cliffs, NJ

Loden, Marylin (1985) *Feminine Leadership* Random House, New York

Manuel, T, S Schefte, D Swiss (1999) *Suiting Themselves: Women's Leadership Styles in Today's Workplace* The Radcliffe Public Policy Institute

Mant, A (1997) *Intelligent Leadership* Allen & Unwin, St Leonard's, New South Wales

McKenna, E P (1997) *When Work Doesn't Work Anymore: Women Work and Identity* Simon & Schuster, London

Moore, T (1992) *Care of the soul.* Piatkus, London

Nicolson, P (1996) *Gender, Power and Organisation: A Psychological Perspective,* Routledge, London

Opportunity 2000: *Benchmarking Report and Index* – Spring 1999

Pascal Blaise (1576) *Pensées* Garnier-Flammarion, Paris 1976

Peters, T (1997) *The Circle of Innovation* Hodder & Stoughton, London

Richardson, J (1996) *Handbook of Qualitative Research Methods for Psychology and the Social Sciences* BPS Books, Leicester

Rosner, J (1990) "Ways women lead" Harvard Business Review November – December

Sellers, P (1999). *"The fifty Most Powerful Women" Fortune*, no. 20 October 25

Segerman-Peck, L (1991) *Networking and Mentoring* Piatkus, London

Stokes, J (1994) What is unconscious in organisations? In R Casemore, G Dyos, A Eden, K Kellner, J McAuley and S Moss (Eds) *What Makes Consultancy Work: Understanding the Dynamics* South Bank University Press, London

Sullivan, Ruth (1999) "Skirting the Issue?" Director, June

Taffinder, P (1995) *The New Leaders: Achieving Corporate Transformation Through Dynamic Leadership* Kogan Page, London

Taffinder, P (1998) *Big Change: a route map for corporate transformation* John Wiley, Chichester

Tait, Ruth (1995) *Roads to the top* Macmillan Press Ltd, Basingstoke, Hants

Tannen, D (1992) *You Just Don't Understand: Women and Men in Conversation.* Virago Press, London

Tannen, D (1996) *Talking from 9 to 5* Virago Press, London

Thomson, P (1995) "Aftermath: making public sector change work – Part 1." *Public Policy Review* Vol. 3, Issue 1

Trompenaars, F (1993) *Riding the Waves of Culture: Understanding Cultural Diversity in Business,* Nicholas Brealey Publishing, London

Vallely, B (1996) *What Women Want: The Campaign for Social and Political Change.* Virago Press, London

White B, Cox C, and Cooper C (1992) *Women's Career Development: A Study of High Flyers* Blackwell Business, Oxford

Wilkinson, H (1994) *No Turning Back: generations and the genderquake.* Demos, London

Wilkinson, H, M Howard et al (1997) *Tomorrow's Women.* Demos, London